Introduction to
American Indian History and Cultures
SECOND EDITION

Robert A. Bell

Kendall Hunt
publishing company

Cover image © Shutterstock, Inc.

Kendall Hunt
publishing company

www.kendallhunt.com
Send all inquiries to:
4050 Westmark Drive
Dubuque, IA 52004-1840

Copyright © 2015, 2019 by Kendall Hunt Publishing Company

ISBN 978-1-5249-9047-3

Published in the United States of America

Table of Contents

Chapter 1 Terminology

Beginning to study Native American history and culture, it is important to become familiar with some terms and general information that will be utilized throughout the course. It is important to note that the word *Indian* did not exist in the Americas until after Christopher Columbus arrived in 1492. When Columbus arrived in the Americas, he really thought he was in the East Indies, so as he and his men came ashore, the inhabitants of the island they had landed on came out to greet Columbus and his men. Columbus mistakenly believing he was in Indonesia named the people he met *Indians*. The name stuck and remains today. Columbus had run into a landmass that he did not realize existed before, and hence a land that was new to the Europeans had been found. Now it is to be remembered that the tribes that existed in the Americas had their own names, but after Columbus named them all *Indians*, that would be what the Europeans and eventually the Americans would forever know the first inhabitants of the Americas as.[1]

The question is raised: which is the best term to use when referring to the first inhabitants living in the Americas? Should they be referred to as Indians, Native Americans, or by some other name? The answer is not an easy one. Some of the original inhabitants prefer to be called Native Americans, others prefer Indians, others prefer American Indians, and most like to be called by their real and original tribal name. A good example of that is in northern Wisconsin and Minnesota, the Indians that live there like to be called by their original tribal name and that is the Anishinaabe, or translated into English means "the people." The non-Indian people that live in this region know the tribes as the Ojibwe, or as the United States government recognizes the tribe as the Chippewa Indians. But the Indian people themselves like to be known as and called Anishinaabe. It is important to remember that each tribe and band has a name, and in the case of many times the Europeans were the ones that named these people. But the Indians prefer to be called by their names before the Europeans arrived.[2]

It is also important to note that before, first the Europeans and later the Americans, tried to colonize the Indian people in the Americas, there were no words like nation, band, tribe, and reservation. The Indians themselves like to be known as "the people" and not be called by a name that was given to them by the Europeans and Americans. These four words are a direct indication as to how complex the relationship is between the Indian people and the United States. But as time wore on, the tribes acquired the names they are known by today. An example would the Red Cliff Band of Lake Superior Chippewa Indians—Red Cliff being the band and Lake Superior Chippewa Indian being the Indian nation. None of these names existed before the arrival of the Europeans, but as time had passed the names and distinction between the tribes were made by the Europeans and now there are 567 differently named federally recognized tribes. As for the Indians, they, as an example the Indians living in Wisconsin and Minnesota, prefer to be called by the name the Creator gave them and that is Anishinaabe.[3]

---

[1]Anton Treuer, *Everything You Wanted to Know About Indians But Were Afraid to Ask* (St. Paul: Borealis Books, 2012), 7.
[2]*Ibid.*, 8–9.
[3]*Ibid.*, 11.

Another term that is associated with Indians is the word Pow-Wow. Many non-Indian people associate this word with the peace treaty making process. This is not true as a Pow-Wow is a social gathering that all people both Indian and non-Indian may attend. This was a stereotype that was created in the old western movies and is a label that has stuck. Toward the end of the class there is one day devoted to the study of Pow-Wows and the dances that are associated with them.[4]

It is now time to go back in time and look at the Indian cultures and civilizations that existed in the Americas before 1492 and the arrival of Columbus. Columbus was lost and did not realize what kind of civilization he had run across in the western hemisphere. That encounter forever changed the lives and life style of the Indians, and although they were very accommodating to the Europeans and Americans their lifestyle and civilization was forever changed and lost for a time but is slowly being rediscovered. The course will attempt to bring to light the civilization that existed and how it was changed. Today, both Indians and non-Indians are trying to tell the real history of the Indians in the Americas and rediscover the cultures that were lost for a time.

Work Cited

Treuer, Anton. *Everything You Wanted to Know About Indians but Were Afraid to Ask.* St. Paul: Borealis Books, 2012.

---

[4]*Ibid.*, 13.

Chapter 2

Native American Cultural Regions

The people that were now populating the continent of North America, whichever direction you believe they crossed the land bridge, were creating their own unique culture. Thus, it is important to examine how the environment influenced each unique culture of each tribe. There are eleven different cultural regions in North America alone, and these eleven are the only ones that will be examined in this class. The regions are the Arctic, sub-Arctic, Northwest Coast, Plateau, California, Great Basin, Southwest, Plains, Western Great Lakes, Northeast, and Southeast. The study of these cultural regions will be done in the proper way that Native American historians, scholars, and archaeologists, use, i.e. west to east. The study will be done traveling west to east as suggested by archaeologists as to the way the people traveled across the land bridge that connected Siberia, crossing the Bering Strait, to Alaska and North America and then migrated, heading first south and then east.

© Wollertz/Shutterstock, Inc.

The Arctic

Most archaeologists believe that as the people from Siberia came across the land bridge, spanning the Bering Strait, chasing their food supply, many became trapped on the east side because of the rising oceans caused by the melting glaciers. According to archaeologists, many of the people that had crossed the land bridge started migrating south to seek a warmer climate and more abundant food sources in the form of plants as well as animals. Some of them, however, decided to stay in the cultural region called the Arctic. Native Americans disagree with this theory as they believe they originated in the Americas and have always lived in the Americas. Native Americans dispute what archaeologists believe about the migration from Siberia and the land bridge.

The Arctic Cultural Region is located along the northern coast of the North American continent. All of the Arctic is located above the Arctic Circle, and the soil is always frozen. The temperatures do not rise above the freezing mark, 32 degrees F, and the angle of the sunlight does not allow for much thawing of the ground. The ground has a special name—permafrost—meaning the ground never thaws, and consequently there is no growing season to grow crops. The landscape of the Arctic is called the tundra. It is a wide-open, windswept land that is flat and has a few small hills on it. There is not a lot of snowfall in the Arctic, but because of the openness of the land the often high and consistent winds cause a lot of drifting of the snow. This creates some very large snowdrifts.[1]

The people that stayed back in the Arctic are called the Eskimos. The Eskimos are the only people that live naturally in the Arctic, and their territory spans from Alaska, all along the north shore of Canada with the Arctic Ocean, to Greenland. They live in one of the harshest climates on earth and have adapted very well to that climate.[2]

© Smit/Shutterstock, Inc.

Eskimos, after first arriving and staying in the Arctic, soon developed and built igloos to live in. They were very ingenious in utilizing the most abundant building material that was available in the Arctic—snow and ice. It is very interesting living in an igloo. One would believe that living in a dwelling made of ice and snow would be very cold inside, but actually it is very warm because snow and ice have very good insulating properties. It is a fact that the heat generated by one candle located in the center of the igloo will keep the inside of the igloo at 40 degrees F. Also, as the inside of the igloo starts to melt or at least form some water on the inside walls, the water freezes back up and actually adds to the insulation of the igloo. Not all Eskimos lived in igloos; some lived in pithouses, which were made of a combination of wood and whalebone. The home would be constructed by first digging a pit in the ground and covering it with both wood scavenged from crates or driftwood that would wash ashore, as there are no trees in the Arctic to make wooden planks. The whalebones would come from the whaling expeditions to hunt whales for food and other resources. The Arctic is a difficult place to live, but the Eskimos were able to adapt and create a way to survive the long winters by creating dwellings with the most abundant and easily available sources to build with.

---

[1]Merwyn S. Garbarino and Robert W. Sasso, *Native American Heritage* (Prospect Heights: Waveland Press, 1994), 102–104.
[2]*Ibid.*, 104–105.

The Eskimos' main source of transportation for many years was the dog sled. Dogs were a vital part of Eskimo life in the Arctic. Today, a bit of modernization has occurred in both the dwellings and transportation. For homes, lumber is brought in to the Eskimo communities and wooden homes are built, and for transportation cars and trucks are used during the short summer months while snowmobiles are utilized during the long winter ones.[3]

The Eskimos have, over the years, utilized whales as their main food source. There were also polar bears, seals, walrus, and many arctic birds that were utilized for food. But the whale was the main source of food, and one whale would feed an entire village for one year. To go whaling, first the leader of the whaling expedition would say a prayer giving thanks to the animal for giving up its life so that the village could live. This is a common tradition not only in Eskimo culture but also in Native American religions, i.e. thanking the animal that was killed for giving its life up for the village in order for the people to survive. The whaling party would set out in little boats called umiaks, which were constructed of driftwood, whale bones, and whale or seal skin. After locating the whale, the men would steer in close enough to harpoon the whale and tie a barrel or some other flotation device to create a drag on the whale's ability to swim to tire it out and then kill it. After the kill was made, the whale would be butchered and every part utilized right down to the bones. The oil, or blubber, would be used as fuel to serve as a lighting source which heated the igloo as well. The oil would thus serve a dual purpose.[4] Whaling is still practiced today by the Eskimo community.

The Eskimos live on a very high-fat diet, as their primary food source is the whale. There are other animals that are utilized, but it is still a very high fat-based diet. The Eskimo work hard and live in such a harsh and cold climate the high-fat diet actually is very beneficial to them. The high-fat diet works as a fuel to help keep their body metabolism at a high rate to utilize the fat calories so as to keep their bodies warm. Their clothes were made of the hides of whales and other animals in the Arctic and had to be airtight to help them stay warm and water resistant to keep the clothes dry in the cold.[5]

In order to keep physical altercations and aggression to a minimum, the Eskimo used song duels. If a person felt that they had been injured in some way, either physically or emotionally, they would challenge the perpetrator to a song duel. This was a competition that was done publicly with a panel of judges. The strategy of song duels has worked very well for many years and is still utilized today, not so much as a way to stop physical altercation but as a competition for money. It is a highly popular pastime during the long winter months.[6]

The Eskimo have adapted to the Arctic very well and have created a Native American culture that was influenced greatly by the environment and climate that existed. They were able to find a food source, create building materials from the tundra, and have a transportation system utilizing the dogs that had accompanied the Eskimo to the North American continent. From here, the northernmost point of Native American culture and civilization, we will see how the Native Americans that moved to the south and east created their cultures and civilizations by utilizing the environment and climate they lived in.

The Sub-Arctic

The sub-Arctic Cultural Region lies just below the Arctic and has a slightly milder climate and the environment is more favorable for a short growing season. The sub-Arctic looks a little bit like the Arctic but with a milder climate. The sub-Arctic stretches across all of central Canada, from present-day British Columbia–Alberta to all around the Hudson Bay to the Atlantic coast and Newfoundland, on the east coast of Canada. It runs north to the Arctic Circle and south to the Great Lakes and the United States–Canadian border. The sub-Arctic contains the Boreal Forest, is the beginning of vegetation regions, and has a short growing season of approximately three months. The sub-Arctic climate is not nearly as harsh as the Arctic and is more populated.[7]

---

[3]*Ibid.*, 104–105, 110, 116.
[4]*Ibid.*, 106–107, 122.
[5]*Ibid.*, 106.
[6]*Ibid.*, 121.
[7]*Ibid.*, 126.

Food sources are more abundant in the sub-Arctic, and a larger variety of food sources are available. The Inuit people are the main inhabitants of the sub-Arctic. The Inuit have a better choice of food sources than the Eskimo of the Arctic. The Inuit are not dependent on the whale and other sea mammals for their food source. Their sources of meat include such animals as squirrels, rabbits, foxes, beavers, caribou, deer, moose, and bear. By far the most abundant and chief source of meat is the caribou as there are vast herds of these animals in this region. The sub-Arctic lies below the permafrost line, allowing for a short growing season for plants. Strawberries, loganberries, and raspberries are common in the sub-Arctic and are collected by the Inuit people. Some other crops that can be grown in the sub-Arctic that do not need extremely long periods of warm weather can be grown as well. Crops such as lettuce, broccoli, cauliflower, and potatoes grow well in the sub-Arctic.[8]

The sub-Arctic is the start of the Boral Forrest, and so there is an abundance of pinewood available for construction. The Inuit live in simple wooden structures that are generally elevated off the ground to control rot because of dampness that comes up through the ground because of the cyclical freezing and thawing of the ground. In the past, in the northernmost parts of the sub-Arctic the Inuit lived in igloos like the Eskimo. They also used tents that resemble tipis, such as the ones the Plains Indians used. The Inuit utilize dogs and snowmobiles like the Eskimo, but because the snow melts for part of the year they can utilize automobiles as well.[9]

© Andris Barbans/Shutterstock, Inc.

It should be noted that the Inuit and other tribes that live in the very southern part of the sub-Arctic around the north shore of the Great Lakes, the Ojibwe, Cree, and Assiniboine, were very much impacted by the European fur traders. This region was invaded by the European fur traders by 1650 and changed the lives of the Indians living in this region forever. The fashion rage in Europe after the European fur traders arrived was to own and wear beaver fur hats. Traders thus began to trap and trade for the pelts of the extremely large beavers that resided in the Upper Great Lakes and the central and southern parts of the sub-Arctic. Eventually, the traders traded European-made goods to the Native Americans for beaver pelts. This arrangement turned out to be beneficial to the Europeans, because the Native Americans knew where the very large beavers lived, and it also benefited the Native Americans for a short while as they gained European goods and technology. This arrangement eventually disadvantaged the Native Americans as the beavers were almost trapped to extinction and the economy, which developed for both the Native Americans and Europeans, died causing

---

[8]*Ibid.*, 126–127.
[9]*Ibid.*, 126–127.

great hardships for the Native Americans. It is important to remember that this region was devastated by the fur trade.[10]

Northwest Coast

The Northwest Coast Cultural Region is located along the Pacific Ocean, running from the southern part of Alaska through Canada and the states of Washington and Oregon to the northern state line of present-day California. It runs inland all across British Columbia to the Alberta province line and to the Cascade Mountain Range in both the present-day states of Oregon and Washington. The Northwest Coast's terrain is jagged and has many steep cliffs along the Pacific coast of the United States and Canada. The region is warm all year round, and during the winter months has a great deal of fog along the coastline as the warm Pacific water meets very cold arctic air coming from the North Pole. With these warm water temperatures warming the air, fog is formed. Further inland, the Canadian Rockies and, in the United States, the Cascade Mountains join to create the eastern boundary of the Northwest Coast.[11]

Several Native Americans tribes inhabit the Northwest Coast, such as the Nootka and Kwakiutl who live in the northern most regions of the Northwest Coast on and near Vancouver Island. These two tribes still follow the lifestyle much the same as that of the Eskimo. Whaling is a large part of their lives and their main source of food. The Tlingit and Haida tribes live in the middle part of the Northwest Coast and account for the majority of the Native American population in the Northwest Coast Cultural Region. Living in the southernmost part of the Northwest Coast are the Chinook. The Chinook, living along the Columbia River in what is now the state of Oregon, were known as great traders. They controlled all of the trade between the other Northwest Coast tribes and the outside world. The Tlingit are the largest tribe residing in the Northwest Coast region, and they have a very interesting lifestyle. Their artwork is well known the world over. Since the Tlingit are the largest and most well-known tribe, they will be used to study the Northwest Coast life and society.[12]

Because of the mild weather and the warm currents of the Pacific Ocean, there is an abundance of food sources for the Tlingit and the other tribes on the Northwest Coast. With the mild temperatures, living along the Northwest Coast it is much easier than living in the Arctic and sub-Arctic. Only the Nootka and Kwakiutl tribes live in more difficult conditions, but even they do not live in a region with climate as severe as the ones where the Eskimo and Inuit live.[13]

The major food source of the Tlingit, and the other tribes of the Northwest Coast, is shellfish and fish. There is an abundant supply of these two staples. A few miles inland, with the mild weather, a growing season occurs that allows for the gathering of berries and other plant sources for food.[14]

The dwellings the Tlingit construct are small houses that are made of cedar, which is abundant because of the vast cedar forests that exist in the Northwest Coast. Cedar is the choice building materials for the homes of the Tlingit, because living on the Northwest Coast is very damp. There is a large amount of rainfall and, with the meeting of warm water and cold air, fog, making for very damp living conditions. Cedar is very moisture resistant and readily available in the Northwest Coast region. Because of the damp climate, the Tlingit and the other tribes of the Northwest Coast make coats and other clothing out of cedar by weaving the cedar into a pattern. They also use sealskin as a raincoat and for clothing owing to the climate is very wet.[15]

The people of the Northwest Coast are not only known for their ability to make waterproof homes, clothing, and boxes but also for their artwork, for which there is a huge market. Many geometric designs and

---

[10]*Ibid.*, 127.
[11]*Ibid.*, 155–156.
[12]*Ibid.*, 166–177.
[13]*Ibid.*, 170–173, 175–177.
[14]*Ibid.*, 166.
[15] *Ibid.*, 160.

representations of the Tlingit religious figures and masks have been prized pieces of art that Europeans and Americans have purchased and collected.[16]

© Andrea Izzotti/Shutterstock, Inc.

The Tlingit and the other tribes on the Northwest Coast are also known for their Totem Poles. Now many non-Native American people that live in other parts of North America are making Totem Poles to honor special family members and family achievements. It is to be remembered that these are copies and a cultural appropriation of the tribes of the Northwest Coast culture and is wrong. I live in Chippewa Falls, Wisconsin, and two families that lived for several years on the Northwest Coast thought it was a great idea to create a Totem Pole to honor certain members of their families and their family achievements. These Totem Poles look very much out of place and give the wrong idea to children as to where and which culture Totem Poles belong. It gives the impression that Native Americans and communities along the Northwest Coast are extinct and that these Indian people do not exist anymore and that it is alright to copy and present Native American culture and religion in a Euro-American way that mimics Native American culture. The Totem Pole has a lot of spiritual meaning to Tlingit communities along the Northwest Coast and is a way to tell who lives in a certain household and the family history and which clans of the tribe dwell within that household.[17] During the late nineteenth and early twentieth centuries, archaeologists took 300 Totem Poles away from the Northwest Coast people and brought them to the University of Toronto in Canada. Here, they studied these Totem Poles and made a display of the 300 Totem Poles at the Science Museum of Toronto. In the late 1990s, these Totem Poles were repatriated to their rightful homes on the Northwest Coast. This was one of many examples of Euro-American culture disrespecting Native American culture.

Valuable artwork and Totem Poles are not the only unique aspect of Northwest Coast culture. The elaborate boats that the Tlingit and other Northwest Coast tribes produce are works of art themselves. The boats that the Tlingit and the other tribes make range from canoes made of cedar to navigate the rivers and streams of the Northwest Coast to very large seafaring boats that have very large animals that are carved on the front of the boat that are used in ceremonies. The ceremonies range from religious ceremonies to ceremonial boats that families use to arrive at a potlatch. The boat that a family will use to go to a potlatch is very decorative and has markings that identify the family.

The potlatch is something like a Pow-Wow that would be given by the tribes in Wisconsin and other parts of the lower forty-eight states of the United States. The potlatch determines a family's social status in

---

[16]*Ibid.*, 165.
[17]*Ibid.*, 159–160.

Northwest Coast culture. The potlatch is hosted by a family in a Tlingit or other tribe's community and is a very elaborate affair. The potlatch will last three to five days and everyone that attends is fed many meals and will receive a gift for attending the potlatch. Food is a very important part of the potlatch. Food and gifts are the central part of the potlatch. The bigger the potlatch, the higher the social standing of a family in the community. The competition is fierce among families in Tlingit and other Northwest Coast tribes to gain social status. It is not uncommon today in potlatches given for participants to receive televisions, washers, and dryers as gifts from the host family. It is also common for families to go into deep debt, and even file bankruptcy, because of hosting a potlatch. The potlatch is a very important part of Northwest Coast culture.[18]

The Plateau

The Plateau Cultural Region is located south of the Northwest Coast and is east of the Rocky Mountains in Canada and east of the Cascade Mountains in the states of Washington and Oregon. The Plateau is at a high elevation and is a large, flat parcel of land that is roughly 5,000 feet above sea level. At its easternmost point, it touches and descends to the level of the Great Plains in Western Montana where the Rocky Mountains begin. The Plateau extends south to California and Nevada. There are several Native American tribes that live in this cultural region. They include the Klamath, Spokan, Yakama, Wallia Wallia, Shuwap, Lillooet, Kalispel, Flathead, Modoc, Umatilla, Shuswap, and the Nez Perce. The Nez Perce is the most well-known tribe that lives on the Plateau. The Klamath are a close second as they are well known for the woven grass baskets they produce.

The Plateau has a very dry climate and is at a high altitude that has a very rugged terrain. There is a desert located in the center of the Plateau. The summers are very hot with afternoon temperatures reaching 100 degrees F. In the middle of the winter, temperatures get very cold, sometimes dipping to lows of –20 degrees F to –30 degrees F below zero. The Plateau is a very dry and barren palace with only a very few rivers and streams. Water is at a minimum, and the tribes that reside on the Plateau know how to conserve water. The Plateau receives very little rainfall and little snowfall during the winter. Extremely strong windy conditions exist on the Plateau because there is little vegetation to act as a windbreaker. Because of the windy conditions during the winters what snow is received is blown around causing deep snowdrifts. The Plateau is known as a transitional zone of climatological areas.[19]

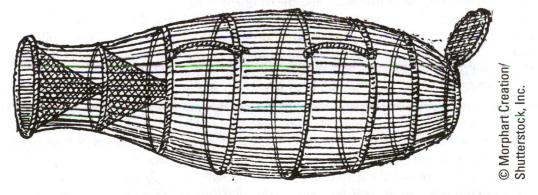

© Morphart Creation/ Shutterstock, Inc.

Because of the arid climate of the Plateau, the food sources that come from the vegetation are limited, and generally these come from the mountains and plains along the edge of the Plateau. The tribes that live on the Plateau gather the numerous berries that grow there and utilize the edible roots of several plants that grow in the desert located in the center of the Plateau. The meat sources include deer and rabbit, though limited in quantity. There are not many rivers that flow through the Plateau. But the rivers that are in the Plateau contain an abundance of salmon. Salmon is the main meat and food source of the tribes that live on the Plateau. The salmon make up for the low numbers of deer and rabbits on the Plateau. The tribes living on the Plateau have developed a unique way to catch the salmon. They use what is called a weir. The weir is a giant fish trap that is

---
[18]*Ibid.*, 162–164.
[19]*Ibid.*, 141.

placed in the swift currents of the few rivers that flow through the Plateau, and as the fish become trapped the Native Americans spear the salmon. It is a very ingenious way to catch the salmon, and it is one of the ways to catch a large amount of salmon to feed an entire village.[20]

The tribes that live on the Plateau are nomadic. They travel all summer following their food sources, the salmon runs, the ripening of berries, and the migration of the deer and rabbits. The Nez Perce is the largest tribe living on the Plateau and was one of the first tribes to utilize the horse after they came in contact with the Spanish. They also had contact with the French fur traders. The Nez Perce were one of the first western tribes that Lewis and Clark met on their Journey of Discovery. The horse helped a great deal as it allowed the tribes to cover a large amount of ground to hunt and gather food supplies. The Nez Perce and other tribes of the Plateau traveled all summer gathering the food for the long winters on the Plateau.[21]

During the summer, the Nez Perce and other tribes of the Plateau utilized tipis. Tipis were used because they are very easy to construct and tear down and were easily attached to a horse and pulled along to the next summer camp. After the tipi is torn down it then can be used as a drag behind a horse. This is called a travois. It becomes a tool to pull behind a horse to place belongings and young children to aid in the transportation from one camp to the next. During the long, cold, and windy winters on the Plateau, the Nez Perce lived in pithouses. These houses were constructed first by digging a hole in the ground. Then logs were used as trusses to support logs and twigs placed over the logs to make a roof. A hole was left in the middle of the roof to allow smoke from the fire, used to both warm the pithouse and cook over, to escape to the outside. These worked well and kept the family living inside warm and dry during the long winters on the Plateau.[22] The tribes living on the Plateau discovered many ingenious ways to utilize what was available in the environment they were living in to survive and create a Native American culture and civilization around this environment and climate.

California

At one point in time before the Europeans arrived in North America, there were over 400 different small tribes living in the area we today recognize as the state of California. California is its own Native American Cultural Region. California is located on the Pacific coast of the western United States and is bordered by Oregon on the north and Mexico on the south. California is divided into three different sections in terms of cultural regions, the northern third, the central third, and the southern third.[23]

Northern California has a rocky coast line with many cliffs. It has the same general appearance of the Northwest Coast but is not as damp. Being located further south, the arctic air does not collide with the warm Pacific waters. There are mountains and deep valleys, and northern California is also the home to the redwood forest. Northern California is located between San Francisco Bay and Oregon.[24]

Numerous Native American tribes reside in northern California. One of the largest tribes is the Pomo Indians. The Pomo, like the other tribes in northern California, are known for weaving very large grass baskets, and that is how they make a living today. The Pomo is a small tribe, and this is commonplace in not only northern California but in California in general. Because of the very mild climate, a long growing season of ten months, and the abundant wildlife, tribes in California did not have to travel far for food, and therefore became sedentary. The tribes did not spread out or intermingle much, so the Native American communities stayed small and did not span out very far, thus creating 400 different tribes before European contact.[25]

---

[20] *Ibid.*, 143–145.
[21] *Ibid.*, 147–149.
[22] *Ibid.*, 150–151.
[23] *Ibid.*, 183.
[24] *Ibid.*, 183.
[25] *Ibid.*, 183–186, 198–202.

© Editor77/Shutterstock, Inc.

As previously stated, the food supply in northern California is abundant, ranging from elk and deer inland to shellfish and fish along the rivers, streams, and the Pacific coastline. One staple that is very consistent in all three cultural zones of California is the acorn. All of the tribes in all the Cultural Regions of California—northern, central, and southern—utilize the acorn. Native Americans make flour and meal out of the acorn to make bread and other food staples from it. There is one drawback to using the acorn, its toxicity. Acorns contain tannic acid that is poisonous to humans. The Native Americans of California devised a way to leach out the tannic acid in the acorns to make for a safe and very nutritious food source. Oak trees that produce acorns are plentiful in all areas of California, and the Native Americans in all regions utilize the acorn.[26]

The California gold rush of 1849 was very disruptive to the Native Americans living in northern California. As miners came into the San Francisco Bay area, the Native Americans were in the way of mining operations. So to control the problem, in 1850 when California became a state, the Governor ordered that a bounty be placed on the Native Americans living in California, especially the northern third. Bounty hunters of Native Americans would receive money for each dead Indian they brought in. This went on until 1902 when the Federal government stepped in to stop the killing. By then however, several northern California tribes had disappeared as a result of the genocide. What happened in northern California for the last half of the nineteenth century is a well-hidden fact in American history.[27]

Central California stretches from the San Francisco Bay area at its northern boundary to just north of present-day Los Angles California. It is almost a carbon copy of northern California. The same food sources are present in an abundant supply. The tribes that live in central California also weave large grass baskets as a way to survive. The Yurok is one of the largest of many tribes residing in central California. Again, there are many small tribes that are sedentary as they do not have to search for food. The tribes of central California utilize the acorn as well since oak trees are plentiful.[28]

Southern California, which spans from just north of present-day Los Angles to the border with Mexico has a terrain and climate that is different. It is dryer and is a desert. It has a very rocky and rugged landscape. The food sources are a bit different than that found in the other two cultural regions, in that rabbits and deer are utilized more than fish, and there is a verity of berries that the Indians utilize. From the few streams and

---

[26]*Ibid.*, 183–188, 198–199.
[27]*Ibid.*, 442.
[28]*Ibid.*, 185, 190–192, 200–201, 442.

lakes, some freshwater fish are taken. But one item is consistent and that is the acorn. Oak trees are abundant in southern California as well, and the acorn is thus one of the main food staples.[29]

In southern California, there are Mission Indians. These are Native Americans who converted to Christianity during the 350 year Spanish occupation of the American Southwest. They received their name because as the Spanish set up missions in the Southwest as they wanted the Native Americans in the area to be more accessible. To do that, they relocated these Native Americans to live either in the mission or right outside the mission. This was done for the following two reasons: (1) to have the Native Americans live with the priests so they would have constant exposure to Christianity, and (2) to have the Native Americans plant and tend the gardens to support both the Indian population now living in and around the mission and to feed the priests. This would be the Native Americans' payment for being saved through Christianity. Mission Indians existed up to the mid-twentieth century.[30]

The Chumash are one of the many tribes that reside in southern California, and because of the dry climate they engaged in more hunting and gathering than the tribes in northern and central California. All of the tribes in southern California lived in villages and did not weave grass baskets. They were more of a hunting and gathering society, even though they were sedentary in nature. They also did not have to go far to find food.[31]

California had the most diversity in terms of the number of tribes, and that is still true today. At its peak, California was home to 10 percent of all of the Native American population in North America, while only accounting for 1 percent of the landmass. At its peak, California also had the densest Native American population; however European contact and the gold rush ended that reign.[32]

The Great Basin

The Great Basin Cultural Region is a dry and desolate area surrounded by mountain ranges. The Great Basin is a very hot place during the summer, with daytime temperatures routinely rising above 100 degrees F; during winter, nighttime temperatures routinely reach –20 degrees F. The Great Basin has little water, and at the floor is a very large desert. The desert is surrounded by mountains, giving the feel of being at the bottom of a giant bowl, hence the name of the region: the Great Basin. The Great Basin receives little rain in the summer and little snowfall during the winter, but the snow is piled into large drifts because of the constant wind that blows across the Great Basin. The Great Basin is a land of climate extremes.[33]

There are several tribes that live in the Great Basin, such as the Ute, Paiute, and Shoshoni, the Shoshoni being the principal tribe in the region. They are nomadic as there really is no land that is capable of supporting sedentary farming. So during the summer months the Shoshoni and the other smaller tribes of the Great Basin move constantly following their food supply. The Shoshoni are also characterized by their horse culture. They became excellent horsemen after the Spanish introduced the horse to this region of North America. Today, the Shoshoni are still known for their ability to raise and train horses, making it a big business for the Shoshoni.[34]

The Great Basin has a limited variety of foods to hunt and gather. Fishing is almost non-existent due to the lack of rivers, streams, and lakes. The main food staple of the Native Americans living in the Great Basin is the Pinion Nut (Pine Nuts). Pinion Nuts give the Native Americans of the Great Basin a high-protein food source. The Shoshoni and other tribes in the region follow the Pinion Nut harvest all summer long. Other food sources include rabbits, mountain sheep, and antelope for meat supply. The people of the Great Basin also utilize the roots of several different plants that grow in this area. They use a tool that their ancestors had developed called the digging stick. This is a stick that is tapered, making it easier to hold on to, and has a rounded

[29]*Ibid.*, 204.
[30]*Ibid.*, 205–206.
[31]*Ibid.*, 204–211.
[32]*Ibid.*, 183.
[33]*Ibid.*, 217–219.
[34]*Ibid.*, 225.

point on the smaller end of the taper. The stick will dig away the dirt at the bottom of the plant allowing the roots to stay intact, and ready for cleaning and processing for storage for the winter as a food source.[35]

© mahirart/Shutterstock, Inc.

During the summer, the inhabitants of the Great Basin utilize the tipi as the dwelling of choice. The tipi is a very useful item for the tribes of the Great Basin because it offers shelter and is easily dissembled and quickly reassembled, something that is important to a nomadic tribe. The tipi while being transported can and is utilized as a carrier of items as it is attached to the horse by the poles that hold up the tipi, and the cover of the tipi is then placed on the poles and then the possessions of the families of the tribes, such as cooking items, are placed on the cover, as are little children. This carrier is called a travois. During the winter months, the inhabitants of the Great Basin live in a dwelling called a Wickiup. It is made of long poles curved into the shape of a half circle. Over the poles brush, matting, and bark strips are used to make the walls. A hole is left in the middle at the top of the half circle to act as a chimney to let the smoke from the warming and cooking fire out of the Wickiup.[36] The Great Basin Cultural Region is one of the most difficult climates and environments to live in on earth. The tribes that live here have developed many different tools and kinds of shelters to survive.

The Southwest

The Southwestern Cultural Region is located in present-day Arizona and New Mexico. This is a mountainous and dry place that is mostly a desert. There is little rainfall, and only a few rivers and lakes are present. The Southwest is home to the Pueblo, Navajo, Apache, and the Hopi tribes. The Anasazi, who were the first sedentary farmers, were the ancestors of the Navajo, Pueblo, and the Hopi. The Pueblo, Navajo, and Hopi are sedentary tribes in the Southwest and still carry on the sedentary farming traditions of their ancestors, the Anasazi, by growing the "Three Sisters." The "Three Sisters" are unique in the way they are grown as they use very little water and feed each other. The "Three Sisters" are corn, beans, and squash. They are planted together and work together to grow. First the corn is planted, and once it emerges the beans are planted on the four sides of the corn, next to the four leaves of the corn that have emerged. Next the squash is planted between the corn and bean plants. The corn acts as a trellis for the beans to grow on and the corn and bean combination provides shade for the squash, which does not thrive in direct sunlight. As they grow together, the waste product of the beans, nitrogen, is discharged into the soil, and this nitrogen is the nutrient the corn needs for its growth. As the squash vines grow over the base of the corn and beans, it keeps the soil moist and smothers out the weeds. This is a very ingenious way to grow crops in the desert and will be examined closer in the next chapter. There

---

[35]*Ibid.*, 217–221.
[36]*Ibid.*, 220.

is one saying among Native Americans: "The 'Three Sisters' want to be together like the Indians want to be together and as long as the "Three Sisters" are together the Indian will never starve." The Anasazi also devised the first irrigation system in North American and possibly in the world, long before European contact.[37]

The Pueblo live in dwellings that resemble apartment buildings, and as the Spanish arrived in the American Southwest, they called these structures pueblos, and that is how the Pueblo got their name. The Pueblo are known for the pottery that they produce. It is very valuable today and much sought after. The Pueblo are excellent negotiators and, in 1680, led a successful revolt against the Spanish. But by 1692, the Spanish reclaimed the territory; their return, however, was on the terms of the Pueblo. The Pueblo have been able to survive the onslaught of European intervention and did not lose their culture. The Spanish also introduced the Pueblo to European animals such as horses and sheep. The Pueblo are not horsemen and nether do they take part in the horse culture, but they raise sheep.[38]

© Nick Fox/Shutterstock, Inc.

The Navajo also live in the Southwest and have many similarities to the Pueblo. The Navajo live in wooden homes built in a hexagon shape called a Hogan. The shape is relevant to their creation story and the entrance always faces east to greet father sun and the day first thing after waking up every morning. The Navajo use a structure called a Kiva as the place to conduct religious ceremonies. The Navajo, like the Pueblo, were not a part of the horse culture that began upon the arrival of the Spanish; instead, they took to raising sheep. These sheep are treated like family members. The Navajo also raise the "Three Sisters" as their main staple food source, and use sheep and lamb as their source of meat. The Navajo also are quite well known for their sand paintings, which form a part of their religion. These are painted in Kivas during religious ceremonies and are erased at the end of the ceremony.[39]

The Hopi also live in the Southwest and are the descendants of the Anasazi. They are closely related to the Pueblo and have many of the same customs and live in adobe apartment-like structures similar to the Pueblo. One major difference is that the Hopi preform what is called the Water Dance, performed by the Katcina Dancers. They would do this to ask for enough rain for a plentiful crop because they live in an arid place.[40]

The Apache are the only nomadic tribe that lives in the Southwest. The Apache are good horsemen and first started working with horses after the Spanish introduced the horse to North America. The Apache use

---

[37]*Ibid.*, 227.
[38]*Ibid.*, 233–238.
[39]*Ibid.*, 248–255.
[40]*Ibid.*, 238–242.

the roots of certain plants in the desert and any berries they can gather; they also hunt rabbits and the small number of deer that live in the Southwest. The Apache are semi-sedentary in that they live in huts made of grass and use that as a home base to return to from hunting trips. Since the weather is warm all year round, the game does not move in advance of the changing of the seasons.[41]

The Southwest has a dry desert climate with a few mountains. It is the home to the first farmers, the Anasazi, and their descendants the Pueblo, Navajo, and Hopi who still live there. They developed the Native American traditional diet of corn, beans, and squash or the "Three Sisters" which is used today to help in both physical and mental healing of Native Americans. The Southwest also saw the start of trade between these communities and other cultural regions. The Southwest was and still is a very important cultural region and could be considered the cradle of Native American civilization.

The Plains

The Plains Cultural Region is located in the very center of North America. The Plains run from the Gulf of Mexico to central Canada, north to south, and east to west from run from the Mississippi River to the Rocky Mountains. The Plains cover the middle one-third of the present-day United States. The Plains is characterized by a very flat terrain covered in grass with very few trees. The lack of trees makes for a very windy climate that sees extreme temperature changes. Because of the location of the Plains, weather fronts tend to collide over this area, causing rapid changing weather conditions and making life on the Plains unpredictable. Before Euro-American settlers came to the Plains, the buffalo was the primary animal that roamed throughout the area following the warm weather. But after settlers moved in, the buffalo herds were killed off and replaced by cattle and sheep.[42]

Several tribes live on the Plains including, the Crow, Comanche, Lakota, Dakota, Nakota, Assiniboine, Arapaho, and the Blackfoot. One of the largest tribes that live on the Plains is the Comanche living in the southern part of the Plains. They are mostly located in present-day Texas and Oklahoma. The largest tribe living in the northern Plains is the Lakota, who reside in present-day North and South Dakota, Nebraska, and Minnesota. Both these tribes were nomadic and followed the buffalo herds until it was hunted to near extinction by the Euro-Americans. All the tribes that live on the Plains have a horse culture. They adapted the horse into their daily lives very effectively, which made hunting and gathering easier. By using the horse, the tribes on the Plains were able to cover more ground per day for hunting and gathering during the summer months to prepare for the long and bitter winter months, especially on the northern Plains.[43]

© iralu/Shutterstock, Inc.

---

[41]*Ibid.*, 246–248.
[42]*Ibid.*, 261–293.
[43]*Ibid.*, 264–266.

The tribes on the Plains live in tipis for the same reason the tribes on the Plateau do, i.e. they are easily torn down and reassembled. They also use the tipi as a drag blanket behind a horse to place their belongings on, and this also serves as a way to transport little children and is called a travois. The tipi is use only during the summer as the winters on the Plains are very cold and windy. During the winter months, the Plains Indians use a more sedentary dwelling, called a lodge, made of the sod from the prairie. This sod is very pliable and insulates very well, making a warm shelter to live in during the very harsh Plains winter. The lodge is circular in shape with a hole in the center at the top to allow smoke from the warming and cooking fire to escape.[44] The Lakota of the northern Plains also utilize the sweat lodge for religious purposes. The lodge is constructed with a circular shape and is covered with buffalo hides and has a fire inside as well as rocks heated in a fire and placed in water to create steam to heat the lodge and make it hot enough for people to sweat. This sweat is a cleansing ceremony to bring one back and closer to the Creator and is a very important of Native American religion on the Plains, Western Great Lakes, and the Northeast.[45]

The food supply of the Plains Indians consists primarily of buffalo meat. But the buffalo is utilized much as the whale is utilized by the Eskimo. The bones, hide, fur, and other parts are used for various activities of daily life. The introduction of the horse made buffalo hunting much easier for the Plains Indians and increased the buffalo kill.[46] The Plains Indians also utilized the "Three Sisters," corn, beans, and squash, along with sunflower seeds as another food source.[47]

One other interesting aspect of Native American life on the Plains is the way an individual's wealth is determined. The wealth is gauged in the two following ways:

1. By the number of horses a man owns. If you have a large number of horses, you are considered wealthy. The father of a daughter who wishes to marry a man would ask that young man how many horses he owns. If the number is too low, then the daughter may not marry this man until he has obtained the proper number of horses to prove that he will be a good provider.
2. By the number of buffalo hides a man owns. By having a large number of buffalo hides, a man proves that he is a great provider and is deserving of any woman's hand in marriage.[48]

The Western Great Lakes

The Western Great Lakes Cultural Region is located around Lake Superior and Lake Michigan, covering present-day eastern Minnesota, Wisconsin, Michigan, Indiana, and Ohio. The Western Great Lakes is a heavily wooded area and the tribes that live in this region used the waterways and rivers as their transportation system. The pine trees that were located in this region were very large, with some having a trunk as large as 10 feet in diameter and standing 100 feet tall. It was easier to use the river than to cut down the trees. The French and English traders and armies that arrived in the mid-seventeenth century discovered that cutting down the trees to make a road was a difficult to near impossible task and was very time consuming.

The Western Great Lakes also have a vast number of rivers, streams, and lakes. The weather in the summer months is generally mild and not overly hot. The winters are generally very snowy, with snow of up to 100 inches sometimes seen. The temperatures can drop to as low as −40 degrees F in mid-winter. The tribes that occupy the Western Great Lakes are the Ojibwe, Menominee, Ho-Chunk, Miami, Illinois, Potawatomi, Huron, Sauk, Fox, and Ottawa.[49]

Food is abundant in the Western Great Lakes. Many berries, such as strawberries, raspberries, and blueberries, grow freely in the region. The "Three Sisters," corn, beans, and squash, are also grown in this area. Deer, bear, elk, fish, and rabbits are plentiful in this region, and so there is no shortage of meat sources of food. There were also many fur-bearing animals in this region which were of great interest to the European traders;

---

[44] *Ibid.*, 266–268.

[45] *Ibid.*, 358.

[46] *Ibid.*, 288–287.

[47] *Ibid.*, 246–248.

[48] *Ibid.*, 272.

[49] *Ibid.*, 319.

hence, this was the most productive region during the peak of the fur trade, from 1650 to 1900. The tribes in the Western Great Lakes, the Ojibwe in particular, also produced maple sugar. They utilized maple sugar as a sweetener, and this was produced in abundance as maple trees were numerous, as were pine trees. The Ojibwe made several products out of the maple sap, including maple sugar, maple syrup, and maple sugar candy.

But the main food source of several of the tribes in the Western Great Lakes is wild rice. This staple contains more protein than most cuts of meat and was easily stored after the harvest. Wild rice is harvested in August in the Western Great Lakes with a birch bark canoe. Two people set out in the canoe; while one steers the canoe through the wild rice slough, the other person uses two sticks called ricing sticks to harvest the wild rice. The person harvesting the wild rice will take one stick and bend the wild rice plant over the center of the canoe, where a blanket or tarp made of birch bark is placed, and gently tap the plant to detach the grain from the stem of the plant. After harvesting all of the wild rice in the slough, the rice is then processed on shore. This is done by first heating and steaming the wild rice and then stomping it, much like Italian vineyard workers stomp grapes for wine, to break open the shell. The wild rice is stored underground to keep it fresh during the winter and until the next harvest. The wild rice can be stored for up to five years and still be as fresh as it was when it was harvested. The tribes that lived in the Western Great Lakes fought over the wild rice as this was the main staple for other tribes apart from the Ojibwe. The Ojibwe and Dakota tribes went to war for 130 years until the Ojibwe drove the Dakota out of the area to present-day Minnesota for the right to have access to the wild rice.

As mentioned earlier, the Ojibwe and other tribes utilized birch bark as a building material. Along with pine and maple trees, birch trees were plentiful in the Western Great Lakes. The Ojibwe in particular made their canoes out of birch bark, because it is waterproof and is easily stripped off of the birch tree. Stripping the bark off the birch tree will not hurt the tree. The bark comes back after a few years, and so the Ojibwe have a building material that replenishes itself. The Ojibwe do not make only canoes out of birch bark, they also cover their lodges with it and make baskets to store things in and cook in. They are able to use baskets made out of birch bark to cook in without the basket catching fire. As stated before, the Ojibwe made their lodges out of birch bark as well, and since it is a good insulating material it creates a warm and dry home during the winter.

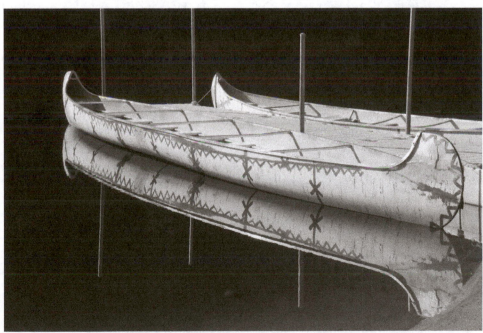

© Leene/Shutterstock, Inc.

The Ojibwe and other tribes in the Western Great Lakes were sedentary and grew crops like the "Three Sisters." The only time the Ojibwe were on the move was during the hunting and fishing seasons. How they did this was to create hunting villages all along the rivers and streams in the region and canoe down the river to them to hunt. There were many hunting villages along the Chippewa and Red Cedar rivers in the Eau Claire area and to the north. The men would set out on a hunting expedition while the women stayed back at the main village of Pahquahwong to tend the gardens. After the European traders arrived and the demand for fur-bearing animals grew, these hunting villages became also fur trapping villages. The birch bark lodges also were used in the sweat ceremonies for the Midewiwin religion that the Ojibwe and other tribes in the region practice. It is very similar to the sweat ceremony followed by the Dakota tribes of the Plains, previously described. The Indians in the Western Great Lakes were very good at figuring out how to use the rivers to and trees to their advantage without cutting all of the trees down.

The Northeast

The Northeast Cultural Region extends from Ohio in the west to the Atlantic Ocean, south to Virginia, and north to Maine and the Great Lakes of Ontario and Erie all the way to Canada. The Northeastern Cultural Region includes the present-day states of Virginia, West Virginia, Maryland, Delaware, New Jersey, Pennsylvania, New York, Massachusetts, Rhode Island, Connecticut, New Hampshire, Vermont, and Maine. The Northeast has the same climate as that of the Western Great Lakes Cultural Region, but it is not as cold during the winter. The daily summertime high temperatures are quite cool while the winters are cold, but rarely do the temperatures go below 0 degrees F. The winters sees a lot of snow, more than is received in the Western Great Lakes. The terrain is much the same with many swift rivers, stream, and lakes that are utilized as a transportation system. It is heavily wooded like the Western Great Lakes with pine, maple, and birch trees. The tribes in the Northeast utilize birch bark in the same manner as the tribes in the Western Great Lakes. They make canoes out of it, and cover their lodges with it as well. The lodges used are very similar to the ones that the tribes of the Western Great Lakes built and used. The tribes of the Northeast also practice religions much like the Ojibwe Midewiwin religion and utilize the sweat lodge covered with birch bark.[50] Some of the tribes that live in the Northeast include all of the members of the Iroquois Confederacy, who will be examined more closely later in this segment, the Seneca, Mohican, Mohawk, Oneida, Cayuga, Onondaga, Tuscarora, Pequot, Wampanoag, and many smaller tribes scattered all throughout the Northeast. The Iroquois and the six tribes that made the Confederacy are by far the best known.[51]

The Iroquois not only live in lodges like the Ojibwe in the Western Great Lakes but also lived in longhouses. These would house up to five families who live in their own cube that was separated from the other families by large woven grass hanging mats. Each family had its own cooking and heating fire in the middle of their compartment, and a hole would be made in the roof above the fire to allow the smoke from the fire to escape. The outer walls were generally covered in thatch and birch bark.

© Zack Frank/Shutterstock, Inc.

---

[50]*Ibid.*, 310–311.
[51]*Ibid.*, 313.

The food sources that the Iroquois utilized are virtually the same food used by the tribes in the Western Great Lakes region. The Iroquois grow the "Three Sisters" and hunted deer for meat. They also gathered berries such as strawberries, raspberries, and blueberries all summer long. These tribes are sedentary as the men go on deer hunts while the women stay at the village and tend to the gardens and gather berries as they come into season. The only difference is there is no wild rice in the Northeast. Wild rice is only found in the Western Great Lakes region.

The Iroquois have one unique cultural aspect compared to all of the tribes of North America, and that is their form of government: the Iroquois Confederacy. This form of government that the Iroquois utilized is very much like the government of the United States. But the Iroquois did not model their form of government after the United States government because the Iroquois Confederacy was founded in the 1370s—122 years before Columbus arrived and 417 years before James Madison wrote the Constitution of the United States. The other unique aspect of the Iroquois is that they did meet regularly and formed laws and rules and even settled disputes between tribes and individuals. They worked together and solved problems. The men that represented each tribe in the Iroquois Confederacy were appointed by the Female Elders of each tribe. Women had a voice and vote in tribal politics and appointed the men they believed would best represent the interests of the tribe. If that man was not doing his job, he was recalled and a new man elected in that position to fight for the best interests of the tribe. This form of government worked very well for the Iroquois, but as Europeans moved in to the Northeast, the Iroquois Confederacy crumbled away as the tribes were eventually removed from their land after 1830.

The other unique aspect of the Iroquois culture is the wampum belt. Wampum is not money as depicted in old 1950s western movies, which is a stereotypical image of Indians and Indian culture. The wampum belts are always purple and white, the purple shells being beads that came from Massachusetts Bay on the Atlantic coast and were made from clamshells. These belts were used as a history book in that they tell the history of the tribe. The wampum belt will depict a big event such as a hunt that was very fruitful. But mostly, these belts would tell when a treaty or an alliance was made and with whom. The wampum belt told the history of the Iroquois and was, and still is, an important part of Iroquois culture.

The Southeast

The Southeastern Cultural Region is a very hot and humid place to live. It is located south of the Ohio River and runs to the Gulf of Mexico and from the Mississippi River to the Atlantic Ocean. The Southeast includes the present-day states of Arkansas, Louisiana, Mississippi, Tennessee, Kentucky, North Carolina, South Carolina, Alabama, Georgia, and Florida. The Southeastern Cultural Region contains many swamps, bayous, and lakes. It is a dangerous place to live as it harbors all of the poisonous snakes that call North America home, as well as alligators. The terrain of the Southeast ranges from mountainous, the southern portion of the Appalachian Mountain Range, to all of the swamps along the Gulf Coast and in Florida, including the Everglades.[52]

The tribes that reside in the Southeast are the Seminole, Cherokee, Choctaw, Chickasaw, and Creek. These five tribes were considered the "Five Civilized Tribes" by the United States government during the late eighteenth and early nineteenth centuries, because they exhibited the ability to alter their tribal civilization and customs and adopt many aspects of Euro-American civilization into their culture. This was both good and bad for both the Indians living in the Southeast. These tribes were sedentary farmers before European contact, and this is the major reason that first the British and later the United States viewed them as civilized.

Food sources were and still are abundant in the Southeast. The tribes in the Southeast grow crops related to the traditional Native American diet, the "Three Sisters," corn, beans, and squash. There are also an abundance of berries, like strawberries, raspberries, and blueberries. Animals like rabbits, deer, and alligators as a source of meat can also be found in the Southeast in abundant numbers. Hunting parties did not have to venture very far from the village to either gather berries and other food staples or to hunt animals for meat.

---

[52]*Ibid.*, 325.

© Mariusz S. Jurgielewicz/Shutterstock, Inc.

The typical housing structure was a thatch hut, which had a frame built of flexible poles covered in grass and thatch. Some thatch huts that were utilized during the day only had grass and thatch on the roof to act as a place to seek shade to get out of the intense heat of the midday sun,. The villages consisted of several thatched huts in close proximity to each other with a tall fence built around the village to keep enemies and predatory animals out of the village. Because of the abundance of water in the Southeast, the Indians used canoes to travel from place to place to trade and harvest food. These canoes were very different from the birch bark canoes of the Western Great Lakes and Northeastern regions. The Indians in the Southeast made dugout canoes. This was a canoe that was made from a log of the cypress tree that was hollowed out and placed in the water. The dugout canoe is not as maneuverable as the birch bark canoe. The Indians in the Southeast do not have access to birch trees and do not harvest wild rice, so they do not need a canoe that is maneuverable.[53] They were a part of the massive trade system that spanned all of the eastern two-thirds of the North American continent.

The Seminole Indians is the most well-known tribe from the Southeast. They live in the Florida Everglades. The reason they live in such a harsh climate and environment is that during the Indian removal period, the United States Army came to force the Seminole out of Florida to move to Oklahoma, and in 1835 most of the tribe fled into the Everglades. A war raged between the United States and the Seminole Nation from 1835 to 1843. The Seminole that did not move to Oklahoma fought valiantly against the United States for eight years, and eventually won. Their victory can be attributed to two facts: (1) the Seminole were very organized in their warfare against the United States and (2) the Seminole utilized the swampy climate, terrain, and variety of natural defenses they had — alligators and over thirty-six varieties of poisonous snakes—to their advantage. The United States gave up in 1843 and the Seminole in Florida still live in the Everglades, and the Everglades was officially reserved for their use, creating the Big Glade Seminole Reservation.[54]

---

[53] *Ibid.*, 328.
[54] *Ibid.*, 337.

Afterword

The examination of the cultural regions of the Native Americans have told how each of the cultural regions have helped to create the customs, culture, and world view of each tribe that lives within that region. Putting all of those regions on to one continent, North America, a diverse yet general culture of Native Americans emerges. There are some cultural and material items that exist in all eleven cultural regions, and every region has cultural and material items that are unique to that region alone. These regions have combined over time to create the Native American culture and civilization seen today and examined in the next chapter.

Work Cited

Garbarino, Merwyn S., and Robert F. Sasso. *Native American Heritage.* Prospect Heights: Waveland Press, 1994.

Chapter 3

Life in the Americas Before Columbus

We will first explore in greater depth the Bering Strait Theory that was briefly discussed at the beginning of Chapter 2. Toward the end of the Glacial Period, around 11,500 years ago, there existed a land bridge that spanned the small strait that is known today as the Bering Strait. Archeologists and anthropologists both agree that the people that were living in Serbia crossed that land bridge following their food supply. As the glaciers melted away the bridge disappeared, and the people that had crossed into North America were trapped on the east side of the bridge that disappeared.

The people then began to follow their food supplies. Some migrated to other regions, while other bands chose to stay where they were, thus leading to the various different tribes that exist today. The migration took several thousands of years to occur, and along the route of the migration some tribes and bands stayed in places they felt comfortable while others kept moving further south and east. This is the theory that anthropologists and archeologists put forth as to how first North America and later, as people migrated farther south and east, the Americas became populated with Native American tribes and communities. This is the scientific explanation as to how the Americas were populated and Native American tribes and communities came into being by the time Columbus and the other Europeans arrived, starting in 1492.

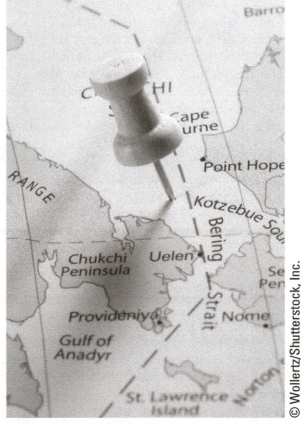

© Wollertz/Shutterstock, Inc.

But the question arises: What do Native Americans believe? Well, Native Americans believe that the land bridge did exist and that people crossed that bridge connecting Asia and North America, but with one small correction. Native Americans believe that the people crossed the bridge going from east to west not west to east. Many Native American scholars believe that the anthropologists and archeologists have the theory backward.

There is validity to what Native American scholars say because every tribe in the Americas, both north and south, have a creation story that places their tribal and ancestral origins in the Americas. For example, there is the story of Winneboozho, part spirit and part mortal, in the Ojibwe creation story. During the great flood, Winneboozho and several animals found themselves clinging to a turtle's back and wondering what to do. The turtle told Winneboozho and the animals that if one of them could dive to the bottom of the flood waters and find some soil they could use his back to create an island to live on. So the bear said that he would dive down since he was the protector of the tribe. The bear dove and was under the water for a long time, but as he reappeared he had failed in his quest. The duck tried next, saying since he was a waterfowl he should be able to fine some soil from the bottom. After a while, the duck resurfaced empty handed. One by one the animals dove down and failed. Finally, the lowly muskrat said he would try. He dove into the water and was gone a very long time. Finally, the muskrat's lifeless body floated to the surface and in his tiny paw there was some soil. Winneboozho formed an island on the turtle's back and that mass is known today as the island of North America. Through the sacrifice of the muskrat, the Anishinaabe people now have a home.[1]

© ArtHeart/Shutterstock, Inc.

But the Ojibwe are not the only tribe that has a creation story having them originate in the Americas. The Oneida have the story of Sky Women. The story begins with the Tree of Life being uprooted in the land of the Sky People. The uprooted tree had left a huge hole in the clouds and Sky Women one day was looking down at the flooded world below. While she is looking through the hole in the sky, her husband came up behind her and startled her causing her to fall through the hole in the sky. Sky Woman grabbed a twig from the Tree of Life as she fell through the hole and four swans arrived to catch her and carry her to safety on the back of the turtle. The story becomes very similar to the Ojibwe creation story as muskrat dives to the bottom and finds some soil. Sky Woman then proceeds to make an island on the turtle's back and she then plants seeds from the Tree of Life, thus creating Mother Earth. Through these two creation stories, Native American scholars say here is evidence that both the Ojibwe and Oneida ancestors lived in the Great Lakes Cultural Region at the time of the glaciers at the end of the Ice Age.[2] Native Americans are able to justify they originated in North American and did not come from Siberia by crossing a land bridge.

The First Farmers

Sometime near the year 2000 BC, the first sedentary farming communities developed. These communities developed in the southwestern part of North America. It is the geographical region of the southwestern region of the United States, the states of New Mexico and Arizona. These people were known as the Anasazi, or the old ones, and were the ancestors of the Hopi, Navajo, and Pueblo tribes that inhabit the southwestern United States today. The Anasazi were the first farmers in the Americas and developed the "Three Sisters."[3] The "Three Sisters" consist of corn, beans, and squash. The Anasazi developed a way to grow these crops in a desert climate. The "Three Sisters" became the traditional Native American diet across the Americas. They also developed irrigation systems to channel water to their gardens. The "Three Sisters" were grown in a unique way to utilize water and shade in a dry and hot climate. First the corn is planted, then the beans are planted with the corn so as the beans grow they will utilize the corn stalk as a trellis to allow the bean plant to grow up the corn stalk while at the same time releasing nitrogen into the soil to feed the corn plant. Beans produce nitrogen naturally as a by-product while growing. The corn and beans are planted 4 feet apart, and the squash is

[1] Patty Loew, *Indian Nations of Wisconsin Histories of Endurance and Renewal* (Madison: Wisconsin Historical Society Press, 2001), 3.
[2] *Ibid.*, 4–5.
[3] Merwyn S. Garbarino and Robert F. Sasso, *Native American Heritage* (Prospect Heights: Waveland Press, 1994), 65.

then planted at 4 foot intervals between the corn and beans. Planting in this manner allows the squash to vine over the roots of the corn and beans, thus keeping the direct sunlight off the roots of the corn and beans, while at the same time trapping the moisture in the soil and smothering out the weeds. This was an ingenious way to grow crops in a desert climate, and the beginning of the Native American civilization that existed before Columbus arrived in 1492. Most archeologists believe that the first farmers, or the Anasazi, began sedentary farming practices sometime around the year 2000 BC.[4]

The Anasazi were not only innovative at farming, they were able to take advantage of the cliffs and rock formations to build their homes. Located in Chaco Canyon, about 100 miles northwest of present-day Albuquerque, New Mexico, lies Pueblo Bonito. At its peak, it is estimated that over 1,000 families lived in the dwellings that were cut into the cliff side. It is believed by archeologists that Pueblo Bonito was built sometime between 900 and 1100 AD and contained 800 rooms, or living quarters for families. Thirty kivas also were contained in this vast settlement. A kiva is a place of worship utilized by the Anasazi at this time and is still utilized by their descendants, the Hopi, Navajo, and Pueblo Indians.[5] Pueblo Bonita also saw the Anasazi create job specialization among its population. This specialization allowed for the creation of skilled craftsmen to create new tools and products to trade with other communities and make farming faster and more efficient. This is the first step in creating a civilization.

© Eric Kukulowicz/Shutterstock, Inc.

But the building by the Anasazi was not confined to building homes and kivas. They built roads that were as long as 400 miles. The main road was 400 miles long and thirty feet wide. The main road contained many branches that connected many small communities to Pueblo Bonito. Thus, a trade network was created. Archeologists have made several discoveries that point to a very large trade network created by the Anasazi that reached as far south as central Mexico and reaching as far east as the Mississippi River. By 1100 AD, a Native American civilization existed. It was a sedentary society that produced crops (primarily the "Three Sisters"), lived in organized communities (Pueblo Bonito), and had established a trade network that was connected by roadways and had a wide reaching influence west of the Mississippi River, in the southwestern region of the North American continent.[6] According to the archeological definition, a civilization is characterized by (1) living in a sedentary setting and growing crops with specialization of jobs for each individual in the community to do thus creating time to make trade items, (2) creating a community that many families live in and creating a central from of government, and (3) creating a trade network connected by roadways allowing trade and communication between many different communities and cultures. By 1100 AD, there existed a Native American civilization in the southwestern United States. A 500-year drought ended the reign of the Anasazi. The drought began to take its toll on the ability of the Anasazi to raise crops for food. They moved from Chaco Canyon and eventually disappeared, but they live on through their descendants the Hopi, Navajo, and Pueblo Indians of today.

---

[4]*Ibid.,* 65.
[5]*Ibid.,* 69.
[6]*Ibid.,* 70.

© William Silver/Shutterstock, Inc.

The Mississippians and Cahokia

While the Anasazi were developing Pueblo Bonito, a culture and civilization was developing along the east of the Mississippi River. The Mississippians were mound builders and at the same time built cities and trade centers along the waterways and rivers of the eastern part of the North American continent. According to archeologists, the building of this trade network and Native American civilization began around the year 3400 BC and became a fully functional civilization by 1250 AD.[7]

Of all of these cities and trade centers that developed, the great city and trade center Cahokia was the largest. By the year 1250 AD, it was probably the largest city in the world. Cahokia was larger than London or Paris, in Europe, at this time and was located on the Mississippi River.[8] The ruins of Cahokia are located east of present-day St. Louis, Missouri in Illinois. It was a very large city with a large population of skilled craftsmen and farmers. The farmers grew the "Three Sisters" like the Anasazi in the southwest, along with a few other crops. Again, it is seen where specialization was present. Some of the population of the city farmed and produced food for the community, thus creating time for certain others to create tools for special purposes to make tasks like farming easier and more productive. But along with the creation of new and more efficient tools came more time to create items to trade with other communities. The trade network thus became very large and prosperous.

The area that Cahokia was located was called the American Bottom because it was located in the backwaters of the Mississippi River in the St. Louis area. A trade network developed in the eastern third of North America that was different from what the Anasazi developed in the southwest utilizing a roadway. Instead the people in Cahokia and the rest of the trade centers from the Mississippi River to the Atlantic Ocean and from the Upper Great Lakes to the Gulf of Mexico utilized the waterways and rivers of this region. This region was very heavily wooded and instead of cutting down all of the trees to create roadways, it was easier to take advantage of the rivers and waterways. They were swift, long, and connected to each other. Using of the birch bark canoe, which was swift and manageable, a vast trade network came into existence along the waterways of the eastern third of North America.

---

[7]Charles C. Mann, *1491* (New York: Vintage Books, 2005), 289.
[8]*Ibid.*, 291–293.

Archeologists have discovered many items that were made in present-day Florida in and around the Upper Great Lakes. Also, archeologists have discovered Lake Superior copper that was mined was made into tools and weapons used as trade items by Ojibwe along the shore of Lake Superior in present-day Wisconsin. Many useful items such as copper pots and arrowheads, have been found in many parts of Florida. There is proof that even the Anasazi and the Mississippians engaged in a small amount of trade among themselves. Some items from each civilization have been discovered in each other's regions.[9]

Basically from the 1100 AD, starting in the southwest and eventually moving east, Native American civilizations began to flourish. It is evident that 392 years before Columbus arrived in the New World there was a Native American civilization that existed and was fully functional. This civilization utilized roadways that were built by the Anasazi in the southwest and a trade network that extended into central Mexico. In the east along the Mississippi River and its tributaries, another trade network existed and grew. The Native American civilizations had at least one city that was larger than any city that existed in Europe during the same time period—Cahokia. Eventually these two trade networks did trade with each other. But, these great empires did disappear. The most important fact to be remembered is the fact that Native American civilizations did exist in the Americas long before Columbus landed on an island in the Caribbean. These civilizations had created a trade network and specialized jobs and had skilled craftsmen to create items to trade and improve life. They had technology that was very different from European technology, but it was technology that Europeans did not have and was very complex and unique. At the time of contact, the Europeans adopted much of the technology that Native Americans had. Things like the "Three Sisters" and the unique way they were grown was a complex way to grow crops that self-fertilize, self-weed, and grow in a hot and dry climate using little water. Native American bows and arrows were something that was highly advanced to anything the Europeans had at the time of contact. Yes the Europeans did have firearms, but at the time of contact a good warrior could shoot accurately ten arrows to one shot from a European gun. Many early Europeans adopted the Native American bows and arrows over their guns as there were at least ten different arrows and at least five different types of bows for different situations. One other technology the Native Americans had that the Europeans did not have was the birch bark canoe. This vessel was highly maneuverable, light-weight, and could handle a very heavy load and not sink or capsize. The early European traders quickly adopted the canoe as they had never seen something so light and easy to carry to portage the rapids in

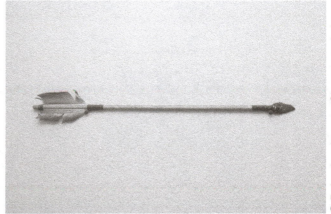

---

[9] *Ibid.*, 295–300.

rivers, and they could also carry a large and heavy load of goods. All of these elements are what make up a civilization, and all of these elements were in place 392 years before the arrival of Columbus and the rest of the Europeans.[10]

Works Cited

Garbarino, Merwyn S., and Robert F. Sasso. *Native American Heritage.* Prospect Heights: Waveland Press, 1994.

Loew, Patty. *Indian Nations of Wisconsin Histories of Endurance and Renewal.* Madison: Wisconsin Historical Society Press, 2001.

Mann, Charles C. *1491.* New York: Vintage Books, 2005.

The Office of the State Archeologist of the State of Iowa, The University of Iowa, web. Accessed April 2015.

---

[10]Office of the State Archeologist of Iowa. The University of Iowa, web. Accessed April 2015.

Chapter 4

First Contact: The Arrival of the Europeans

October 12, 1492 was a day that changed the lives of all Native Americans living in the Americas. As Christopher Columbus came ashore on an island in the Caribbean, he was met by many curious and friendly Native Americans. Thinking he had landed in India or at least the East Indies, or an island chain in the Indian Ocean, he called the Natives he met "Indians." The name Columbus gave the Native Americans he met "Indians" has stuck and was never changed.[1]

Columbus was an adventurer, as were most of the early Spanish and Portuguese explorers and sailors in the late fifteenth century. After Henry the Navigator, a Portuguese sailor, had refined the art of navigation, both the Spanish and Portuguese had started looking for a way to trade with China and India without trading through the Muslim middlemen in the Middle East. The Portuguese had eventually discovered the route around the tip of Africa, called the Cape of Good Horn. But instead of entering that race, Columbus convinced King Fernand and Queen Isabella of Spain that he could reach India and China by sailing west. Columbus was funded by the Spanish government and given three ships and enough workers to man those ships.[2]

© Marzolino/Shutterstock, Inc.

---

[1]Anton Treuer. *Everything You Wanted to Know About Indians But Were Afraid to Ask* (St. Paul: Borealis Books, 2012), 7.
[2]Peter N. Stearns. *World Civilizations The Global Experience*, seventh edition. (Boston: Pearson Publishing, 2015), 507–508.

Columbus began his journey, and after three long months at sea, facing several storms, traversing uncharted waters, and losing one ship and its crew, Columbus and his remaining men landed on an island in the Caribbean. As Columbus and his men were greeted by the Native Americans, Columbus was given gifts. One of the gifts was gold. Columbus left a few of his men as he returned to Spain to show Fernand and Isabella the riches he had discovered in the New World. Upon his return to the Caribbean, Columbus discovered that the Native Americans had killed all of the men he had left, and most of the Native American population had died. Shortly after Columbus started his return voyage to Spain, many of the Native Americans became ill and died of European diseases. The Native Americans became very frightened and placed blame on the sailors that Columbus had left behind. The Native Americans believed the sailors were the reason for the deaths and so killed the Europeans that were left by Columbus.[3]

As Columbus returned, he now wanted as many riches as he could carry from this newfound land. Columbus began to enslave the Native Americans, and if they did not bring him gold or enough riches from the land he would have their hands cut off. These acts by Columbus were only the beginning of many cruel acts of mistreatment and slavery carried out by the Spanish and Portuguese in Mexico and South America.[4]

The Doctrine of Discovery

As the Spanish and Portuguese were conquering the world and finding new landmasses and people, something had to be done to keep these European powers from going to war with each other or more than one country making claim to the same territory. The first action to help prevent wars from breaking out and multiple claims to the same land territory was the Line of Demarcation. The line was determined by Pope Alexander VI in 1493, dividing the world between Spain and Portugal. Everything to the west of the line was Spanish territory and to the east of the line was Portuguese territory, according to a treaty called The Treaty of Tordesillas.[5]

Next came the Doctrine of Discovery. Because there were people living on the land that was now being claimed in the Americas, many explorers needed a statement that would allow them to take the land in the name of the country they were exploring for. Again, it was the Church that decided the fate of the land and the original inhabitants of that land. These decisions greatly influenced the relationship between the Native Americans and the Europeans. This doctrine gave the European governments and the men commissioned to explore and claim new lands for these governments the right to claim the land as it was not developed. It was decreed by the Church that the inhabitants living there had not laid claim to the land and did not claim individual ownership to the land or did not know how to best utilize the land, that it was the right and the will of God that the Europeans take over that land and develop it to its full potential. This was the justification the Europeans needed and used to claim land that many Native American tribes called home. The Doctrine of Discovery had been utilized in many court cases involving Native American claims to land. Many times in the nineteenth century, this doctrine was the basis for removing Native Americans from their ancestral lands and allowing Euro-American settlement. It has to be understood that Native Americans have a very different view on land and land ownership. Native Americans view land as a gift from the Creator that was given to them as a gift to tend and earn a livelihood. Therefore, since the land was a gift and the source from which Native Americans get life, land is not something one individual can own. The land was given as a gift to all Native Americans, so land is possessed by all or it is something that is held communally by Native Americans.[6]

---

[3] *Ibid.*, 508.
[4] *Ibid.*, 508.
[5] *Ibid.*, 219–520.
[6] David Wilkins, *The Legal Universe*, (Golden: Fulcrum Books, 2011), 121–122.

The Pilgrims and Wampanoag

In North America, by 1607, the settlement of Jamestown was established by the British. The early relations between the British and the local tribes in Virginia were not the friendliest, and thus the story of Pocahontas came into being. Pocahontas was not an Indian princess as many tales say. At the time she saved Captain John Smith's life, Pocahontas was only eleven years old and she did not marry Smith. Most historians believe the story of saving the life of Smith as told by Smith is not true. Pocahontas married John Rolfe, a Virginia tobacco planter, and in 1616 sailed to England. Pocahontas was married at age eleven. As the Rolfes were preparing to sail home to Virginia, Pocahontas became ill and died in England. She was buried in England, never returning to Virginia. The story of Pocahontas is one of many stories that have developed as myths over time as to how the first contact between the English or European settlers and the Native Americans living in these areas occurred.

But in the area now referred to as New England, something else was occurring on first contact between the Pilgrims and the Wampanoag. The Pilgrims arrived in New England in the early fall of 1620. They had initially landed on the tip of Cape Cod, but found the area uninhabitable. Eventually by December 1620, the Pilgrims found a better place to settle. As the men went ashore to explore the area, they came upon an abandoned Wampanoag village that had been empty since 1617. Three years prior to 1620, some European sailors or explores had traveled through this part of New England and left several European diseases behind. The Wampanoag became very ill and ninety percent of the tribe living at this village, the Patuxet, died. Massasoit, the chief of the Wampanoag, decided that the tribe should move further inland to escape the spirits or evil that was killing his people.[7]

The Pilgrims viewed finding a village that was cleared of the original inhabitants as God smiling on their endeavor and it was His will for the Pilgrims to live here. Massasoit and the Wampanoag watched the Pilgrims over the winter of 1620 to 1621, and debated what to do about the Pilgrims. Many of the other tribal leaders of the Wampanoag want to finish off the Pilgrims and not have an unknown entity as a neighbor. At this point time, the Wampanoag could have easily killed the Pilgrims and would no longer have to worry about the new settlers. But Massasoit took a different view. Massasoit told his men to watch the Pilgrims and report any suspicious activity. Massasoit was confused by the Pilgrims as these strangers had arrived in Patuxet with women and children. One other aspect that made Massasoit believe the Pilgrims were not a threat was the fact that they were struggling trying to survive. The Wampanoag and Massasoit watched through the winter as nearly half of the people that had arrived died. Massasoit decided as spring 1621 arrived that these strangers were no threat and could possibly be a solution for a problem that Massasoit and the Wampanoag were facing.[8]

By March 1621, Massasoit decided it was time to visit the newcomers and find out if they were friendly or not. As Massasoit sent one of his men into the village with gifts to give and try to meet with the newcomers, the brave was met with suspicion. Soon the Pilgrims realized the Wampanoag meant no harm and wanted to become friends and talk. Massasoit refused to enter the village until a hostage was sent to be held while Massasoit met with the leader of the Pilgrims. Edward Winslow was selected to be the hostage and was sent out. Once Winslow was held captive, Massasoit then went into the Pilgrim village to talk to the governor of the settlement—Jonathan Carver.[9]

[7]PBS, *The American Experience: After the Mayflower*, 2009.
[8]*Ibid.*
[9]*Ibid.*

© Michael Sean O'Leary/Shutterstock, Inc.

Now Massasoit and several of his men entered Plymouth, the name the Pilgrims gave the old Wampanoag village of Patuxet. Massasoit was accompanied by an Indian from New England named Squanto. Squanto had been captured by the Spanish many years ago and sold into slavery in Europe. Squanto had spent some time in England and learned some English. Eventually, Squanto found his way back to New England and found a home with the Wampanoag. Massasoit did not trust Squanto and had him watched at all times by one of the Wampanoag braves.

As Massasoit and his translator Squanto sat down in the center of the village of Plymouth, Jonathan Carver represented the Pilgrims. Both sides agreed to help each other. The Pilgrims only wanted assurance that the Wampanoag would not attack them, and Massasoit agreed stating that he had observed the struggles they were having. But in return, Massasoit asked that the Pilgrims help the Wampanoag if they were attacked by one of their rival tribes in the New England area. Because of their weakened state from the disease outbreak in 1617, the Wampanoag had not recovered in numbers, and still had sporadic outbreaks of disease. Both sides agreed, and the next day Massasoit sent some of the Wampanoag to Patuxet to help the Pilgrims plant corn. The next twenty years were filled with mutual cultural exchange that was friendly and peaceful.[10]

The First Thanksgiving

The late summer and early fall of 1621 found the Pilgrims setting aside a day to give thanks for God smiling on their endeavor. Massasoit and the Wampanoag were not invited to this celebration. It is interesting that the people that helped and promised not to attack or harm the Pilgrims were excluded from this celebration. Massasoit heard gunshots and became concerned that either the Narraganset or the Massachusett Indians were attacking the Pilgrims. So Massasoit and a few of his men went to Plymouth to see what was going on. Upon arriving, it was observed that the Pilgrims were having a celebration and the gunshots heard were only shot as part of the celebration and no hostilities were occurring from the surrounding tribes. The arrival of the Massasoit and his men caught the Pilgrims off guard and they were a little embarrassed because the Pilgrims had not invited the Wampanoag to this Thanksgiving celebration. Governor Carver and Edward Winslow then proceeded to invite the Wampanoag to the celebration, but they were short on food.[11] The Wampanoag

---

[10]Charles Mann. *1491,* (New York: Vintage Books, 2005), 33–35.
[11]Michelle Tirado, *The Wampanoag Side of the First Thanksgiving Story,* Indian Country Today Digital Indigenous News November 23, 2011. https://newsmaven.io/Indiancountrytoday/archive/

went back to their village and brought with them five freshly killed deer and other foods. The celebration that was to be only be an afternoon of giving thanks to God for smiling on the Pilgrims' endeavor turned into a celebration that lasted for three days. It was not so much the fellowship and food that was important that came from this celebration, but rather the show of respect between the leaders of the two parties. Massasoit and Winslow respected each other and became very good friends until Winslow's death in the 1640s. The agreement that was made in the spring of 1621 lasted for only nine years.[12]

© Everett Historical/Shutterstock, Inc.

Now it is to be remembered that the Thanksgiving holiday that is celebrated today is not something that came from the celebration in 1621. The Pilgrims, and eventually the Puritans, only had occasional days of thanks. The celebration in Plymouth in the late summer–early fall 1621 was not a celebration that became an annual celebration.

It was not until 1863 that Thanksgiving became an American holiday. After Abraham Lincoln gave the Gettysburg Address on November 19, 1863, he proclaimed a National Day of Thanks. After Lincoln spoke at Gettysburg, he made a presidential proclamation that the fourth Thursday in November would be set aside annually as a National Day of Thanks. In 1863, the National Day of hanks had another meaning and that was to thank God that the Union had won the battle of Gettysburg and Lincoln believed a National Day of Thanks would take the minds of the people living in the Union States off the American Civil War. The National Day of Thanks was not a day that people had off, as is the tradition today. But it was a day on which everyone was to give thanks to God for all of the blessings that existed in America.[13]

The Thanksgiving holiday that is celebrated today started in 1934. Under pressure from the owner of Macy's department store in New York City, President Franklin D. Roosevelt declared that Thanksgiving become a federally recognized holiday and that it be a four-day-long holiday. Roosevelt moved the holiday back one week, declaring that the third Thursday in November be the Thanksgiving weekend holiday. The reason Macy's department store's owner and the Macy family wanted Thanksgiving to be a federally recognized

---

[12]PBS, *The American Experience: After the Mayflower*, 2009.
[13]Roy P. Basler ed. *Collected Works of Abraham Lincoln* "Proclamation of Thanksgiving", Abraham Lincoln Online.

holiday and last four days was because in 1934 the United States was in the middle of the Great Depression. Macy figured that if people had time off from work and his store sponsored a parade that introduced the holiday season and brought Santa Clause to town, people if they had any money would have the time and be in a festive mood and would spend what money they had on gifts for Christmas. In the Macy families' eyes, this was a way to lead America out of the Great Depression.[14]

There are many myths about the Thanksgiving holiday, but the original day of thanks the Pilgrims celebrated in 1621 really was not the basis of the celebration. After the Thanksgiving celebration in 1863 during the American Civil War, the Pilgrims and Indians did not appear in the lore of the celebration until 1890, for no apparent reason. Thanksgiving is celebrated only as a day of thanks stemming from the dark days of the American Civil War and the start of the Christmas shopping season, a thought from the Great Depression as a way to stimulate the economy.

The Puritans and King Philip's War

In 1630, a ship was anchored off the coast of Massachusetts. Its cargo was 1,000 Puritans, with a charter to create the Massachusetts Bay Colony of Great Britain. Soon the agreement between Massasoit and Jonathan Carver was forgotten. The Wampanoag were still very susceptible to European diseases and their numbers still were in decline. But the ship that arrived in 1630 with the Puritans was only the beginning. By 1640, there were 20,000 Puritans living in New England, compared to only 300 Pilgrims and Puritans living in the area in 1622. In the early 1640s, Edward Winslow died and the friendship and warm relations with the Pilgrims was soon forgotten as a younger generation began to view the Indians in a different light and as a group of people that were in the way of the progress and growth heralded by the arrival of the Puritans.[15]

With the population growth of the Puritans, the Wampanoag and other tribes living in the area were still becoming sick with the diseases the Europeans brought with them. The Puritans viewed the death of the Indians as a blessing from God, clearing the way for their settlement of this new land and that God was giving his chosen people a place to live. The new attitude of the Puritans soon became a major problem for the Wampanoag and other tribes living in New England as these tribes were now viewed as a people in the way of progress and in the way of trade and growth.[16]

By 1637, the Puritans had become the major power in New England. During that year, the Puritans also identified another power in the region that was impeding the expansion of the Massachusetts Bay Colony, the Pequot tribe residing between the colony and the Connecticut River. The colony was losing trade to the Dutch, so the Pequot had to be dealt with. In 1637, the Puritans went to war with the Pequot and killed the entire tribe. Massasoit was very disturbed by the tactic used by the Puritans. At the end of the Pequot War, the Puritans burned a fort to the ground. Within the fort were 700 Pequot, including men, women, and children. In Indian society, killing women and children was unheard of.[17]

It is to be noted that before European contact, such acts as killing women and children was not commonplace among all tribes in the Americas. Violent acts like scalping, beheading, and dismembering a body was unheard of. These types of acts were few and far between in the Americas before the arrival of the Europeans. The Europeans taught the Indians how to commit these acts, and it was learned by the Indians because, as the Indians became allies with Europeans, in order to receive a bounty, the Europeans had to have proof of the death of the enemy. Also, the Europeans brought the practice of bringing home war trophies of cut-off hands, fingers, and other body parts. It is ironic that these people of God and the chosen people of God were so violent and savage. Native American civilization was much more civil than the civilization of the Europeans.[18]

---

[14]Lily Rothman. *FDR Moved Thanksgiving to Gove People More Time to Shop*, Time Magazine, http://time.com/3603622/fdr-moved-thanksgiving/ (accessed July 24, 2018).

[15]PBS, *The American Experience: After the Mayflower*, 2009.

[16]*Ibid.*

[17]*Ibid.*

[18]*Ibid.*

During the 1650s, the Puritans began places known as praying towns. The purpose of these towns was to convert the local Indians to Christianity. The Indians had to cut their hair and dress like the English as they were told that in the Bible it was wrong to have long hair. The cutting of the hair was a traumatic experience for the Indians as an Indian only cuts his hair when in mourning or that individual has had some sort of failure in life. The cut hair points out to the rest of the tribe that something is not right. By the 1660s, half of the Indians living in New England were living in praying towns. These Indians did miss the old traditional ways and were not comfortable with the new lifestyle that was being forced upon them through the assimilation policies of the Puritans.[19]

After the Pequot War, the Puritans were making a statement to the Indians that "do not cross our path or get in the way of our progress". Before he died, Massasoit had seen, over forty years, his original agreement with the Pilgrims completely crumble and questioned his judgment back in 1621. Because of the praying towns, Massasoit now banned the Christian Missionaries from entering Wampanoag villages. The reasoning behind this was the Wampanoag were now beginning to lose their cultural values and assimilate into English society. Massasoit wanted to stop this and try to keep the Wampanoag culture alive. In the mid-1660s, Massasoit died and his son Metacon became chief of the Wampanoag. Metacon also wanted to keep the Wampanoag traditions and culture alive and so kept the ban on missionaries in place after he became the leader of the Wampanoag.[20]

Massasoit's son, Metacon, was also known as Philip and had many friends that were both English and Wampanoag. He spoke English as well as Wampanoag. Philip had many riches and was a proud man, and acquired the name among the English as King Philip. By 1674, Philip saw the Wampanoag being pushed off their land and being treated as second-class citizens within the land they had always called home. He began to amass firearms to prepare to go to war with the English. Philip had many misgivings about going to war with the English, but the misgiving that stood out the most was going against his father's (Massasoit), promise to Carver to not harm the English or make war upon them from fifty years earlier. But these were different times and different people now.[21]

Winslow's son Josiah Winslow was now governor of the Plymouth Colony and wanted to end the problem of the Indians being in the way of expansion. Josiah Winslow called for a meeting with Philip and accused Philip and the Wampanoag of preparing to make war on the Puritans. Philip and the men that accompanied him to the meeting with Winslow turned over their firearms to the Puritans and left. Philip continued in secret to amass firearms and created alliances with other tribes in the area. On June 20, 1675, war broke out with the Indians from several tribes attacking Puritan villages. By December 1675, the 500 Indians living in the praying towns were removed from those towns by the Puritans, because the Puritans no longer trusted any Indians because of the war. The Puritans took the Praying Indians to Deer Island, which was located in the middle of the Charles River and left them there with no food and shelter. All of them died a miserable death by starving and freezing to death.[22]

The war lasted until 1676 when finally the Iroquois Indians made a surprise attack on the Wampanoag killing half of the Wampanoag population. Eventually, Philip was captured and killed by the Puritans. A Praying Indian named John Alderman shot and killed Philip and the Puritans and then dismembered Philip's body and spread these parts of Philip's body to the four corners of the Massachusetts Bay Colony. Alderman was given Philip's right hand as a trophy for his service in the war. The Puritans then took Philip's head and placed it on the end of a pole. The Puritans then erected that pole in the center of the Village of Plymouth and left it there for twenty years, as a reminder to the Indians still living in the area that the Puritans were in charge in New England and this would be the way the Puritans would handle any rebellion against them. A question to think about after reading the story of the first contact and following fifty years: Who were the savage and uncivilized people in this story?[23]

---

[19]*Ibid.*

[20]*Ibid.*

[21]*Ibid.*

[22]*Ibid.*

[23]*Ibid.*

Works Cited

Basler, Roy P. ed. *Collected Works of Abraham Lincoln* "Proclamation of Thanksgiving," Abraham Lincoln Online (accessed July 24, 2018).

Mann, Charles. *1491,* New York: Vintage Books, 2005.

PBS Video, *The American Experience: After the Mayflower,* 2009.

Rothman, Lily. *FDR Moved Thanksgiving to Gove People More Time to Shop,* Time Magazine. http://time.com/3603622/fdr-moved-thanksgiving/ (accessed July 24, 2018).

Stearns, Peter N. *World Civilizations the Global Experience,* seventh edition. Boston: Pearson Publishing, 2015.

Tirado, Michelle. *The Wampanoag Side of the First Thanksgiving Story,* Indian Country Today Digital Indigenous News, November 23, 2011. https://newsmaven.io/Indiancountrytoday/archive/ (accessed July 24, 2018).

Treuer, Anton. *Everything You Wanted to Know About Indians But Were Afraid to Ask,* St. Paul: Borealis Books, 2012.

Wilkins, David. *The Legal Universe,* Golden: Fulcrum Books, 2011.

Chapter 5

Changing Times

The fur trade brought many changes in Native American society. There were many positive changes to Native American culture, such as the addition of metal pots and knives that made everyday life much easier. But the fur trade had just as many negative effects as positive. Some of the effects included rivalry among tribes to trade with the Europeans and a growing dependency up the Europeans for goods and substance in order to survive. Many chiefs, after over 100 years into the fur trade, stated that they wished they had never gotten involved with the Europeans in a trading society as the Indians had become dependent on the Europeans and the trade involved. Here is the beginning of the decline of Native American traditional ways and culture. Many cultural values and traditions were lost because of the fur trade.

The fur trade began in 1650 in the Western Great Lakes Cultural Region as French missionaries and traders arrive at La Pointe Island (today Madeline Island in northern Wisconsin). The fur trade also was beginning in other parts of North America, along the eastern seaboard. The extremely large beaver offered much fur to work with and to help fuel the newest fashion statement in London and Paris in the mid-seventeenth century, the beaver pelt hat. The fashion statement continued well into the nineteenth century, and had devastating effects on Native Americans and their traditional way of life. At first early in the fur trade, many Native American tribes found the fact that they were able to trade very old and worn-out beaver fur coats they possessed for many labor-saving items such as metal pots, metal knives, and fire arms to mention only a few. The tribes could not believe how high a price the Europeans placed on a worn-out beaver pelt coat.[1]

The size of the beaver that was living in the Northeaster and Upper Great Lakes regions were enormous. These animals were the size of a German Sheppard dog and they were abundant as Native Americans used them only for the fur and used the beaver in a conservative manner. Soon, the supply of old worn-out beaver pelt coats depleted and the need for more trapping of beaver became necessary. As the demand for the beaver pelts increased, the Native Americans needed to begin to trap the beaver at a higher rate. How the Native Americans trapped the beaver is unique and very dangerous as well. The Native Americans would build a live trap near a beaver lodge and create a run for the beaver to follow when they were chased out of their lodge. The beaver would become trapped in the trap and then would have to be removed alive and then killed so as not to damage the fur. Removing the beaver was a tremendous challenge as the beaver would fight, bite, and claw the person removing the beaver form the

---

[1]Richard White, *The Middle Ground: Indians, Empires, and Republics in the Great Lakes Region 1650–1815* (New York: Cambridge University Press, 1991), 94–98.

trap. There are many written records describing the number of cuts, scratches, bite marks, and claw marks on the individuals involved in the live trapping during the fur trade.[2]

The ability to trade an old worn-out beaver pelt coat was the only positive that came out of the fur trade for Native Americans. It was a dangerous endeavor to trap beavers as they were large animals and fought very hard while being removed from the traps. Many people were injured participating in this part of the fur trade. But there were other negatives as well. The fur trade cause many rivalries among tribes to gain favor with the Europeans and eventually the Americans.

The early seventeenth century saw the beginning of one of the bloodiest and violent wars between Native American tribes in North America. It is called the Iroquois Wars or the Beaver Wars. The war started over the fact that the beaver population in western New York was beginning to become depleted. The extremely large beavers had all been trapped out and only smaller animals remained and it took two to three of them to equal the larger beaver that was trapped in the beginning. The British demanded more furs and told the Iroquois to move on north into French and Huron Indian territory. The British also told the Iroquois to attack and kill as many of the Huron Indians as they could because the Huron were allied with the French and the British wanted to keep the French influence weak in North America. Here is the first time Native American tribes were drawn into a conflict between two European Imperial powers. The Iroquois nearly annihilated the entire Huron tribe and killed many French as well. The war progressed into present-day Wisconsin, both in terms of battle and refugees fleeing the Iroquois. The Western Great Lakes region is where the war stopped and the Iroquois made a retreat back to New York. The war had nearly eliminated the Huron tribe, and several tribes in the Western Great Lakes region were badly bruised from the war. The French were weakened in their North American possessions. During the mid- to late seventeenth century, 1650–1690, the British used Native American tribe to their advantage against the French and, vice versa, the French used, but not as effectively as the British, the Indians against the British. This was the first time in North America that Indian tribes were used as allies to European powers and against each other in conflicts where for the most part the tribes had nothing at stake or anything to gain but favored status with either the British or the French.[3]

As trade was becoming more established, especially along the south shore of Lake Superior, the Europeans had to learn to deal with the women of each tribe. The British had to do this in the east as well. We will concentrate on the south shore of Lake Superior. The Europeans discovered an important part of Native American culture at this juncture, and that was the importance and power of Native American women. Women in Native American society have a lot of political power and are the traders for the tribe. Women have a high status in the tribe and became a very important part of the fur trade. Within the tribal governments women were allowed to vote and pick men to represent the tribe in meetings with other tribes to work either differences or trade agreements. The European men that came to the Americas to attain riches through the fur trade did not know how to deal with the tribal setup. They really did not want to deal with the women of the tribes because European women did not have a high status in European society like Native American women did within their tribes.[4]

Soon the European traders figured out how to best utilize the status Native American women had within their tribes. The traders began to marry the Native American women to gain a foothold within that village. The traders generally married a chief's daughter. Going down the rivers, as all Native American villages are located along the major waterways in the eastern woodlands, it was not uncommon to discover that a European trader had eight or nine wives in eight to nine different villages to gain control of very large areas of the south of Lake Superior. These unions brought something else with them and that was mixed-blood children. These children were called metis people and during the fur trade they were very important people. Metis people could speak both a European language and Native American languages. At this time, these people became important as they could navigate between both worlds.[5]

---

[2] *Jesuit News* Wisconsin Historical Society Website (accessed February 10, 2012).
[3] Patty Loew. *Indian Nations of Wisconsin Histories of Endurance and Renewal* (Madison: Wisconsin Historical Society Press, 2013) 122, 138.
[4] White, Chapter 3.
[5] *Ibid.*

The fur trade brought many changes to the Native Americans. Some were good like metal pots, knives, and fire arms. But the negatives were many. Once Native Americans became too reliant on European goods and after 100 years of trading furs, Native Americans began to lose some of their traditional and cultural ways. The rivalry between tribes caused many conflicts that had never happened before. Lastly, the fur trade introduced a new type of person—the metis people. Metis people were important until the fur trade died out, after the fur trade ended they were not very respected in the white world or the Native American world.

© Oleksandr Berezko/Shutterstock, Inc.

The French and Indian War

As France and England became bigger European Imperial rivals, they forced Native American tribes to choose sides in conflicts that the tribes had nothing to gain from. These conflicts caused much scarring, and bad relations between tribes still exist today.

The French needed allies as they did not have many French citizens or military presence in North America. In 1740, the French conducted a census of all the Indian villages within New France, to determine how many Indian men they could count on to help the French if and when am Imperial War would break out between France and England. The census was an extensive project but produced dividends for the French as the French and Indian War broke out in 1754. The Indians that fought in the French and Indian War had nothing at stake in this war but only their allegiance to either France or England. The war only intensified wounds and rivalries that began during the fur trade.[6]

By 1761, the war had concluded after the French surrendered to the British at the Plains of Abraham along the St. Lawrence River at present-day Quebec City in Canada. The Seven Years War, as the conflict was called in Europe, came officially to an end in 1763, with the Treaty of Paris. The terms of the peace were that France would give up all of her land possessions in North America, but would be able to hold on to her possessions in the Caribbean. The tribes that France was allied with since 1650 felt betrayed by the French and really did not want to have to deal with the British as they preferred the French as a trade partner. The tribes now were at the mercy of the British and did not trust the British and did not trust any Europeans after the Seven Years War. After the conflict, many of the tribes that were involved decided that maybe it would be best to stay out of any European conflicts in the future.[7]

The American Revolution

By 1774, problems were arising between the American colonists and the British Crown. The Indian tribes in the east, particularly in western New York and the Iroquois Confederacy, decided that if a conflict were to break out between the American colonists and Great Britain they would stay out of the conflict. The Six Nations of the Iroquois Confederacy viewed the problems and hostilities that were developing between the British and Americans, as a family squabble, a rebellious child (the Americans) and its parent (the British). [8]

---

[6]*Ibid.*, 94–95.
[7]*Ibid.*, 119–128.
[8]History Matters. *The War for Independence through Seneca Eyes: Mary Jemison Views the Revolution, 1775–79*, http://historymatters .gmu.edu/d/5826 (accessed May 2012).

War did break out between the Americans and the British in April 1775, and until 1778 the Six Nations were very successful at staying out of the conflict. The American Revolution had only been three years old when the British approached the Seneca for help. The British were bogged down in another war in India and their best Generals were in India and not in North America. More British troops were being dispatched to India than the American Colonies, leading to many bad choices and lack of leadership by the British during the American Revolution.[9]

The British convinced the Seneca that the Americans were untrustworthy and that they should help the British as the Seneca already knew how the Great Father in Britain had treated the Seneca in the past and would continue to treat them after the rebellion was put down. Cornplanter, the Seneca chief at the time, reluctantly decided to help the British, but this alliance came with a cost. The Seneca split over joining forces with the British, with half of the tribe moving to Canada in protest over the alliance. The ones that moved to Canada did not want to enter the conflict at all in fear that if the Americans did win the war, they would punish the Six Nations for fighting for and alongside the British. Not only did that half of the Seneca move to Canada, many of the other members of the Six Nations moved as well. For the Six Nations Tribes that allied and fought with the British in the American Revolution, things went very well with many successful raids on the American Army and American civilians living on the western frontier.[10]

By late summer and early fall 1779, George Washington summoned General John L. Sullivan and gave him a mission. Sullivan was to attack the Seneca and other tribes in western New York to cripple them in their alliance with the British. He mission came to be known as Sullivan's Raids and this was the first attempted genocide of any Indian tribe by an American Army. Sullivan was to take out the food supply of primarily the Seneca and other tribes of the Six Nations that were helping the British. Sullivan's Army arrived in the easternmost villages of Seneca and the American Army's target was the fruit trees, corn harvest, and the civilian population, which was old men, women, and children. The idea was to attack this portion of the population while the warriors were away fighting the Americans for the British. Sullivan's Army cut down all of the fruit trees and burned them, then set their sights on the crops in the fields. These crops were burned before they could be harvested and the stored crops were either thrown into rivers or just thrown about. When Sullivan reached the largest Seneca village on the Genesee River, in mid to late October 1779, the villagers had fled the village before Sullivan arrived. Once in the village Sullivan's men destroyed all of the dwellings and fruit trees and burned them. The crops that were left standing in the fields were burned, and the stored corn supply was thrown into the Genesee River and what could not be thrown into the river was burned.[11]

The members of the village now had nowhere to go or any food for the winter. They decided to go to Fort Niagara and see if the British would give them sanctuary. As the Seneca refugees began their trip to the west, it began to snow. The snow was coming early and nobody could have imagined how big and bad of a storm was coming. The Seneca had to walk through snow that in many places was 5 feet deep. The Seneca finally arrived at Fort Niagara, and the British allowed them to stay during the winter. This was the first time the Americans used food as a weapon against Native Americans as a way to control them. This will not be the last time we will see this tactic used against Native Americans.[12]

The Treaty of Greenville and Tecumseh's Confederation

Shortly after the American Revolution ended, the young country needed to expand to accommodate a growing population. So the newly formed government sought to negotiate land cession treaties. Land cession treaties are treaties that are negotiated between two parties, in this case Native American tribes and the United States government, to acquire land for a determined price in both money and goods. These treaties were negotiated by the military for the United States as the Indian Department was part of the War Department in the early years of the United States government. The negotiations were normally short as the men negotiating for the

---

[9]Peter N. Stearns. *World Civilizations the Global Experience*, seventh edition. (Boston: Pearson Publishing, 2015), 639.
[10]History Matters.
[11]Winona LaDuke, *Recovering the Sacred The Power of Naming and Claiming*, (Cambridge: South End Press), 154–156.
[12]History Matters.

United States would generally find a chief of one of the tribes involved in the negotiations and pressure him to sign for many tribes.[13]

This strategy was evident at the negotiations for the Treaty of Greenville in 1795. The parcel of land in question was a large tract that includes today most of the state of Ohio and the southeastern portion of Indiana. There were nine tribes involved in these negotiations, and representing the United States was George Rodgers Clark and General Anthony Wayne. There was a great deal of discussion over the terms and amount of land to be given up and a lot of discussion among the tribes involved as to who would decide to agree to the terms of the treaty. Finally one chief decided he was going to speak for all without a general consensus of agreement among all of the tribes present and signed away all of the land of all nine tribes. [14]

The incident outraged many Indians in Ohio, Indiana, and Kentucky, and thus a movement to band together began to form to have a general consensus of agreement among all of the tribes involved before any more land cessions were to be made. At this point in time, the fur trade was winding down and with more and more tribes being moved to the west there was not enough land to support the Indians and many men were unable to feed their families. The United States also was taking advantage of this situation by incorporating the factory system into the fur trade that was still working in the Northwest Territories. The factory system worked in this way, a Federal trade post would be established in a region as a place for Indians to trade furs for items such as metal pots and pans, firearms, cloth, beads and other items. The Indians were extended a line of credit for the year and at the end of that year the Indians would bring the furs they had accumulated for trade to pay for the goods they had purchased on credit. Every time there was not enough in the furs to cover the debt, the Indian would have to pay the rest or the fulfill debt through a land cession to the trader. This was a way for the United States to gain more land without making a land cession treaty. Since Indians view land a communal property of the tribe, the giving up of the land just to be able to feed your family was very difficult to take. The fur trade had moved many people on to small tracts of land that could not sustain the population. Also in may villages because of the wars with the United States and other tribes over the right to trade with the United States, there were very few men in these villages, and many times there were four times the number of women over men in the villages. Alcoholism now became a new problem among the tribes because of the depression that had overcome many men of the tribes.[15]

At this time, 1805, Tenskwatawa, or the Prophet as he became known by the Shawnee tribe of which he was a member, awoke from a drunken stupor with a message for all of the Native Americas. The Prophet was one of the men in the tribes pushed into the Northwest Territory who was unable to feed his family and relied heavily on his brother Tecumseh to help him feed his family, as Tecumseh was a great hunter and warrior. Tenskwatawa while drunk had passed out and fell into the cooking fire in the home of his family. His wife pulled him form the fire and the entire village took him for dead. A few days later, Tenskwatawa awoke form his coma and told how the Master of Life (Shawnee name for God) had come to him and gave him a message to preach to all of the Indians. The Master of Life told him to tell the Indians to forsake the white man's way. They told him the Indian was not to live that way, that the Indians had their own civilization, and hence was not to live the way of the whites. The Master of Life also told Tenskwatawa that all the Indian people were to leave alcohol alone and not partake of it, as alcohol was an evil of the white man and was very bad for the Indian people. The Indian people were to go back to the traditional ways of their ancestors and to be kind to each other and help each other out.[16]

Over the course of the next two years, the Prophet's message caught on and many Indian people from many different tribes came to hear him speak. Tecumseh, the Prophet's brother, watched the crowds grow that came to listen to the Prophet, and was amazed that the message had a polarizing effect on the Indian people and united them across tribal lines. The polarizing effect was something Tecumseh was looking for as a way to unite all of the Indian people across the tribal lines to become one united Indian Nation to work at stopping the westward advancement of the Americans. The next five years would see Tecumseh and the Prophet not only give the message of reform from the ways of the whites, and forsake alcohol and become pure again in the traditional

---

[13]White, 469–473.
[14]*Ibid.*
[15]PBS. *We Shall Remain: Tecumseh's Vision.* 2009.
[16]*Ibid.*

ways of their ancestors, but also added that the Indians now needed to stand together as one nation.[17] This is the beginning of pan-Indianism or thinking of yourself as first Native American and tribal affiliation second. Joseph Brandt was the first Native American to talk about this, and Tecumseh carried on this conversation.

The two brothers set up an Indian town in what is today Battlefield Indiana. The town, by 1811, housed nearly 15,000 Indians from many different tribes and was called Prophetstown. Tecumseh finally had what he wanted and that was united front that would collaborate future land cessions and he was advocating that the land north of the Ohio River to Canada and the land east of the Mississippi River to the Ohio River in the east to be given to all of the tribes and called the United Indian Nation. Tecumseh did not stand alone, the British were helping him acquire firearms as the young United States and Great Britain were about to go to war again. Tecumseh was allying with the British, and General Isaac Brock assured Tecumseh that if the Indians and British were to win the war and they believed they would Great Britain would set aside land for Tecumseh's United Indian Nation the land they wanted to become their own sovereign Indian nation.[18] Native Americans define sovereignty as inherent sovereignty which means the Indians have the right to govern themselves and control their destiny from generation to generation and that this was a right was given to them by the Creator through nature.

During late October 1811, the Territorial Governor of the Indiana Territory, William Henry Harrison, became very worried about the large number of Indians gathering at Prophetstown and hurriedly found a Miami Chief that would secure his signature on the controversial land cession treaty the Treaty of Fort Wayne. The chief signed for seven tribes and outraged Tecumseh, who threatened to kill the Miami chief. The following week, Harrison and Tecumseh met in Vincennes, the capital of the Indiana Territory. The meeting was very tense and Tecumseh stated his case as to the way any further land cession treaties would be handled by the Indians: consensus among the Indian leaders and not having one chief sign for many. Tecumseh also told Harrison that he represented all the Indians on the continent and was given consent to speak for them. Tecumseh also informed Harrison that he was heading on a recruiting mission in the southeast to try to muster more interest in the Indian Confederacy that was housed at Prophetstown and that he was trying to have more tribes enter Prophetstown. That news made Harrison even more nervous about the large Indian population moving into the Indiana Territory and he began to believe the situation was going to have to be handled with military action.[19]

© Everett Historical/Shutterstock, Inc.

---

[17]*Ibid.*
[18]*Ibid.*
[19]*Ibid.*

As Tecumseh was leaving the meeting with Harrison to head to Mississippi and Alabama to talk to the Choctaw, Creek, and Chickasaw Indians, he told the Prophet that whatever he did not to attack Harrison under any circumstances while Tecumseh was away. Wait until Tecumseh returned to do anything militarily because Tecumseh was a brilliant military tactician. Unfortunately for Tecumseh and the Prophet, Harrison had started to move a military force north toward Prophetstown. By the evening of November 6, 1811, Harrison and his army was camped 2 miles from Prophetstown where a creek merged with the Tippecanoe River. In Prophetstown, many chiefs and headmen began to pressure Tenskwatawa to attack Harrison before he attacked them, Finally, Tenskwatawa gave in and at 4:30 a.m. on the morning of November 7, 1811 all of the Indians living in Prophetstown came charging out of the fog of that morning and the Battle of Tippecanoe began. At first, the Indians had great success, and with surprise on their side the battle was going their way. Just before the attack, Tenskwatawa told his warriors to be sure to shoot and kill the man on the white horse as that will be Harrison because he rides a white horse. As the Indians attacked Harrison's encampment his white horse ran off, frightened and he took his second in command's brown horse. Harrison's second in command tracked down Harrison's white horse and mounted it only to be promptly killed. The Indians believed they had killed Harrison, but that was not the case as Harrison rallied his men and routed the Indians. Harrison proceeded to chase the Indians out of Prophetstown and he and his men burned the buildings to the ground along with burning and destroying the food supply that was stored in Prophetstown.[20]

Tecumseh was very angry with his brother upon his return from the southeast. But Tecumseh rallied the Indians together and formed an alliance with the British. The Battle of Tippecanoe was the first battle of the War of 1812. The only aspect that is taught about the War of 1812 in secondary schools is the Battle of Lake Erie, Fort McHenry, the burning of Washington D.C., and the Battle of New Orleans. In the west where Tecumseh and Isaac Brock were teamed up, the alliance captured eight forts. Success in the western war ended in late September 1813 when Brock was killed at the Battle of Fort Niagara. That loss made it harder for Tecumseh and his army as the new commander, Henry Proctor, was not interested in the alliance with the Indians and in countless battles after the death of Brock, the British simply left the field and left the Indians in very vulnerable situations. Finally on October 5, 1813, during the Battle of Themes River in Ontario Canada, the battle turned against the British and Indians. The British again left the field and left the Indians in a hopeless situation. Tecumseh was shot and killed during this battle, and this was the end of the Indian Confederacy and Tecumseh's vision of a United Indian State. Many historians believe that if Tecumseh had not been killed, the war in the west would have ended differently and we here in Wisconsin, Michigan, Illinois, Indiana, and Ohio would be an Independent Sovereign Indian Nation today.[21]

Works Cited

History Matters. *The War for Independence through Seneca Eyes: Mary Jemison Views the Revolution, 1775–79.* http://historymatters.gmu.edu/d/5826 (accessed May 2012).

Jesuit News. Wisconsin Historical Society Website (accessed February 10, 2012).

La Duke, Winona. *Recovering the Sacred: The Power of Naming and Claiming.* Cambridge: South End Press, 2005.

Loew, Patty. *Indian Nations of Wisconsin Histories of Endurance and Renewal,* Madison: Wisconsin Historical Society Press, 2013.

PBS Video. *We Shall Remain: Tecumseh's Vision.* 2009.

Stearns, Peter N. *World Civilizations the Global Experience,* seventh edition. Boston: Pearson Publishing, 2015.

White, Richard. *The Middle Ground: Indians, Empires, and Republics in the Great Lakes Region 1650–1815.* New York: Cambridge University Press, 1991.

---

[20]*Ibid.*
[21]*Ibid.*

Chapter 6

Indian Removal and the Trail of Tears

After the War of 1812, many tribes were pushed out and moved farther west. By the mid to late 1820s, Indian removal was becoming something that was commonplace. From the use of land cession treaties to land cession through the factory system, Indians were being forced away from their homelands into areas where other tribes lived, and with the increase in population hunting for food or making a living through the fur trade was becoming near impossible. Life became very difficult for Indians after the 1828 election of Andrew Jackson as president of the United States, as Jackson's main objective during his tenure as president of the United States was to remove all the Indians living east of the Mississippi River to the Indian Territory he set aside for the eastern Indians to be removed to.

Jackson was a frontiersman from Tennessee. Jackson was born and raised in North Carolina and grew up during the American Revolution. During his younger years, Jackson grew to have a dislike of Indians. It is not really known as to why he developed this dislike, but as time passed his hatred toward Indians grew. As a young man, Jackson decided to seek his fortune by moving west, along with many frontiersmen and fortune seekers, and settled in Nashville, Tennessee. There he became a country lawyer and land speculator. He acquired a fortune in money through land speculation. As Indian tribes in western Tennessee sold land through land cession treaties, Jackson would enter the process by purchasing the Indian land from the U.S. government for as low as $100.00 for 2,500 acres and turn around and sell it for $5,000.00. Jackson profited greatly form the Indian land cessions.[1]

© Everett - Art/Shutterstock, Inc.

During the War of 1812, Jackson's dislike of Indians became very obvious. Jackson had brought together many of his fellow frontiersman in western Tennessee to form a militia unit from Tennessee, commonly known as the Tennessee Volunteers. During his campaign in Alabama, against the British and their ally the Creek Indians, Jackson had heard of an attack by the Creek Indians on a settlement of Americans, killing all 200. Jackson was outraged at this atrocity and vowed that he and his Tennessee Volunteers would make the Creek Tribe pay dearly for the massacre. Jackson and his men tracked the Creek Indians and located all 800 of the Creek Indians at a fort located at a place called Horseshoe Bend on a river in Alabama. There, Jackson and his men attacked and brutally defeated the Creek Indians, killing all 800. After the battle, Jackson and his men then proceeded to skin all of the Creek Indians and made bridles for their horses from that skin. By doing this, Jackson was able to exhibit just how

---

[1]Ronald Takaki. *A Different Mirror: A History of Multicultural America* (New York: Little, Brown and Company, 2008), 79.

much he hated Indians, and this attitude would definitely did not disappear after he became the president of the United States.[2]

Jackson's agenda after he was elected president became evident early in his administration as one of the first acts that was passed was the Indian Removal Act of 1830. The act simply stated that all of the Five Civilized Tribes, the Cherokee, Creek, Choctaw, Chickasaw, and Seminole, were to be removed to a new land that Jackson had set aside, called the Indian Territory, today the state of Oklahoma. Some Indians took the offer right away and voluntarily moved to the new Indian Territory. But the rest stayed and the Cherokee, in particular, decided to fight the Indian Removal Act through the U.S. court system.[3]

The Cherokee and the other five tribes living in the southeastern United States had long been recognized, first by the British and later by the Americans, as civilized Indian tribes that had a life style that very much resembled Euro-American culture. One fact about the Five Civilized Tribes in the southeast that set them apart from other Indian tribes was that they were sedentary farmers, and were sedentary farmers when first the Europeans arrived and then the Americans. Because of their life style, they had not been removed yet as they were important to some of the economy of the old south.[4]

The Cherokee could attribute some of their life style to a man named Major Ridge. Ridge had fought in the American Revolution for the British. After the Americans had won the war and took over ownership of the southeastern region of North America, Major Ridge saw the Americans treat the Cherokee and the other Five Civilized Tribes very badly. Ridge saw the importance of creating a Cherokee civilization and lifestyle that resembled the Americans. But before Major Ridge began to seek that type of life style for the Cherokee, a man named Sequoyah created the Cherokee alphabet and the written Cherokee language. Sequoyah believed that one of the major advantages and weapons the Americans had over the Cherokee and other Native American tribes was the ability to write their languages down. Shortly after the Cherokee alphabet came into existence, a weekly newspaper written in both Cherokee and English began to be printed. The newspaper began to make the Cherokee look more American. There were other adjustments to Cherokee culture, such as the ownership of African American slaves, Christianity being practiced by almost all Cherokee, developing a more precise sedentary farming system, and taking individual ownership of land just like the Americans. The Cherokee prospered and looked very American. The Cherokee also had a written Constitution modeled after

---

[2]*Ibid.*, 80.
[3]*Ibid.*, 81.
[4]PBS. *We Shall Remain: The Trail Tears.* 2009.

the Constitution of the United States and had placed exact boundaries around their nation and called it the Sovereign Cherokee Nation.[5]

But not all of the Cherokee benefited from the cultural changes. Only the top 8 percent actually benefited. They became very wealthy and created a lifestyle that was modeled after the plantation culture of the old slave-holding south. The other 92 percent of the Cherokee had not seen any benefit of the life style, and for the first time in Native American history was there now a class system within the Cherokee Nation. The members of the lower classes worked as servants for the top 8 percent as paid help, not slave help. The lower class in Cherokee society really believed the top 8 percent had lost all Cherokee cultural values and was not looking out for the best interests of all of the Cherokee people. This change led to something that had never been seen in Native American civilization before and that was a class system.[6]

One other item that the Cherokee took advantage of was schooling their children in the way of the white man. In 1819, the U.S. Congress appropriated $10,000.00 annually, through an act called the Civilization Act, toward the education of Native Americans. The money was used to educate Indians using church missionaries placed within the Indian Nations to teach them civilization, small things such as the use of tableware, eating at regular times, and dressing more like an American. Major Ridge saw this as the opportunity he was looking for. He sent his son John Ridge and nephew Elias Boudinot to the Missionary University in Connecticut. John turned out to be a brilliant student but had a very cold and distant personality. Elias was not as good a student but possessed a much warmer personality. Both studied American law as this was what Major Ridge believed would help the Cherokee to not be removed and stay in their ancestral land. While at university, John fell in love with the daughter of one of the staff and eventually was able to win over her parents, despite being Cherokee, and they were married just before John was to return home after graduating. At their wedding, a mob of angry white people gathered to protest the marriage. John Ridge now began to question the Cherokee idea of looking more American and acting more like white people. Ridge from this day forward looked at white people in a different way and came to believe that no matter how many customs and traditions of white people that Indians would adopt, Indians would never be able to look and act enough like white people to be fully accepted into white society.[7]

The other family that was important within the Cherokee Nation was the Ross family. John Ross was part Cherokee through his mother, while his father was a Scottish trader, which ran the trade post within the Cherokee Nation. What John Ridge lacked in personality, John Ross made up for. Being metis made it easier for John Ross to navigate both the world of the Cherokee and the Americas. Eventually, this fact will be very important to the Cherokee Nation.[8]

As John Ross became a man, his popularity and trust among the Cherokee grew. Major Ridge took the young man under his wing as John Ross became active in Cherokee Nation politics. It was John Ross that wrote the Cherokee Constitution, which was modeled after the U.S. Constitution. After the adoption of the Cherokee Constitution, the Cherokee now had the ability to fight any removal attempts as now the United States had to treat them as a sovereign nation. John Ridge doing the legal work and John Ross speaking, as he was a much better speaker than Ridge, decided to fight Andrew Jackson's Indian Removal Act through the American court system. It was going to be very important to do this as the State of Georgia desperately want the Cherokee land located within the State of Georgia because cotton was becoming a major export crop and Georgia and the rest of the deep American south had hit an all-time high in price. Coupled with the discovery of gold in 1828 within the Cherokee Nation, the need for Cherokee land was fueled even more. When the Cherokee adopted their Constitution, many legislators stated that they needed to do something fast as if the Cherokee become recognized as the Cherokee Nation that they would never be able to rid Georgia of the Cherokee.[9]

John Ross and John Ridge decided to challenge Andrew Jackson in court with the *Cherokee Nation vs. the State of Georgia*. In 1830, the case reached the U.S. Supreme Court. The case was denied a hearing as the Justices decided an Indian Nation challenging a state had no grounds. But another case *Worchester vs. the State of Georgia*

---

[5]*Ibid.*
[6]*Ibid.*
[7]*Ibid.*
[8]Ibid.
[9]*Ibid.*

came before the Justices of the U.S. Supreme Court shortly after the *Cherokee Nation vs. the State of Georgia* was denied a hearing. *Worchester vs. the State of Georgia* was a case involving Daniel Worchester, a missionary working within the Cherokee Nation. After the Indian Removal Act was passed and the Cherokee were put on alert that they were going to be removed and become subject to Georgia state law, the State of Georgia arrested Worchester under a Georgia law that stated non-Indians were not allowed to be within any Indian land including the Cherokee Nation as that nation was inside the Georgia state line and Georgia did not recognize the sovereign Cherokee Nation. Worchester believed his civil rights had been violated as he believed the State of Georgia could not extend and exercise her state laws and statutes within a sovereign Cherokee Nation.[10]

The case was heard by the Supreme Court, and Chief Justice John Marshall gave this ruling. The Cherokee Nation is a very different and special Indian Nation in that it resembles the American civilization and they have a Constitution like the United States. Marshall went on to rule in favor of Worchester and the Cherokee Nation by stating that the State of Georgia or for that fact any state cannot extend it laws or statutes into a sovereign Indian Nation as Indians are considered a sovereign people by the U.S. Constitution. The ruling of 1832 by John Marshall set up this order of governmental power in the United States:

1. The Federal Government
2. Tribal Government
3. State Government
4. Local Government[11]

The Cherokee Nation was ecstatic with this ruling, but President Jackson was not at all happy with it. Jackson said that it was John Marshall who made that ruling and so let him enforce it. In other words, Jackson decided to look the other way and informed the State of Georgia that the state could do whatever it needed to do to move the Cherokee out. The State of Mississippi did not waste any time removing the Choctaw in the northern part of the state. The Mississippi legislature informed the Choctaw that they were no longer recognized as a tribe and that if they wanted to stay in Mississippi they would have to purchase the land they were living on and were now subject to any state taxes. The Choctaw were thus forced to leave Mississippi, and the State of Mississippi and the Federal government had already moved in 7,000 troops to help the Choctaw move to the newly established Indian Territory. The move, commonly called the Trail of Tears, occurred during the winter months of 1830–1831. Many died along the way due to starvation and being exposed to the elements.[12]

Meanwhile something had to be done about the Cherokee, as the Supreme Court ruling directly affected them. Jackson's Secretary of War told the president not to worry. The Secretary was a veteran of the negotiations during the 1790s and knew that sooner or later one of the Cherokee leaders would crack and agree to a new treaty that would cede all the Cherokee Nation to the United States and force the Cherokee Nation to move to Indian Territory. By December 1835, a weak chief was found and negotiated a treaty with the United States against the authority of the Cherokee Chief John Ross that divided the Cherokee Tribal government, people, and nation. The Federal government negotiated with Major Ridge and his son without John Ridge and the rest of the Tribal Council. On December 29, 1835, the Treaty of Echota was signed and a few days later the U.S.

---

[10]*Ibid.*

[11]David Wilkins. *The Legal Universe*, (Golden: Fulcrum Press, 2011) 129–137.

[12]Takaki, 83–87.

Senate ratified the Treaty of Echota by one vote. The treaty became U.S. law which called for the removal of the Cherokee to Indian Territory west of the Mississippi River by May 23, 1838. Many Cherokee believed the Ridge family had sold them out. Many now questioned why they made all these changes and cultural losses just to have the man that instilled those changes negotiate and sign a treaty of removal of the Cherokee with the United States behind their backs and without the approval of Chief Ross and the Tribal Council. Just after New Year 1836, Major Ridge and his family left for the Indian Territory.[13]

John Ross decided to stay and fight the Treaty of Echota because it was narrowly passed the U.S. Senate, just by one vote. Ross came up with a petition drive, and every Cherokee that was residing in the Cherokee Nation signed the petition—15,665 Cherokee. In early May 1838, a sympathetic United Senator to the Cherokee cause to fight removal was to present the petition to the full Senate. But the day before it was to be presented, two Congressmen had a duel and one of them was killed. Congress adjourned and the deadline of May 23, 1838 passed. On May 26, 1838, members of the Georgia militia and the U.S. Army began rounding up the Cherokee and placing them in staging camps to prepare for the journey west. As the Cherokee left, citizens of the State of Georgia quickly moved into the old Cherokee Nation and laid claim to the land.[14]

© JNix/Shutterstock, Inc.

The first Cherokee that walked to Indian Territory had great difficulty as this was the warm and disease-prone time of the year. John Ross convinced the Federal authorities to delay the departure of the rest until mid to late October to let the disease-prone time pass. In late October, the mass migration began. No one could have foreseen that the winter of 1838–1839 would be one of the snowiest and coldest on record. John Ross had personally bought enough supplies for the move, three months' worth, but because of the harshness of the winter and ice on the rivers a three-month journey became a six-month one. Many Cherokee died of starvation, exposure to the cold and snow, and disease. They finally arrived in Indian Territory by the spring of 1839 and rebuilt their nation.[15]

There was much blame going around, and not long after the move John Ridge, Elias Boudinot, and Major Ridge were all killed in one day. Someone had to pay for the 400 plus lives that were lost during the journey to Indian Territory. John Ridge went on to become Chief of the Cherokee for forty years and help to build a strong new Cherokee Nation in the Indian Territory. The new Cherokee Nation fought internally for twenty-five years, but emerged stronger than before. The Cherokee had the best education system in the

---

[13]PBS. *We Shall Remain: The Trail Tears.* 2009.
[14]*Ibid.*
[15]*Ibid.*

United States at one time. Shortly after the American Civil War, John Ross would see the United States wanting to take more land from the Cherokee. Ross died in Washington, D.C., fighting to keep the new land the Cherokee were now living in. They were successful at keeping their new nation intact.[16]

Works Cited

PBS Video. *We Shall Remain: The Trail Tears.* 2009.
Takaki, Ronald. *A Different Mirror: A History of Multicultural America.* New York: Little Brown and Company, 2008.
Wilkins, David. *The Legal Universe.* Golden: Fulcrum Books, 2011.

---

[16]*Ibid.*

Chapter 7

The Ending of Resistance on the Plains and U.S. Assimilation Policy

In 1851, the time for the United States to put an end to fighting among the tribes living on the Plains had come. The Lakota, Crow, and other tribes on the Plains had to stop warring with each other so the United States could guarantee the safety of the settlers and miners that were passing through or settling to start farming near the Indian Territory on the northern Plains.[1]

The Fort Laramie Treaty of 1851 came about because of this rising problem. The United States called together the headmen of each tribe at Fort Laramie in the Wyoming Territory. The treaty was a treaty with little to no negotiation between the Lakota, Crow, and other tribes on the Plains, instead the United States knew what it needed from these tribes and basically dictated the terms to the tribes. There also was a major change as to how any negotiation process was to proceed. Instead of several chiefs representing each faction of the tribe, the Fort Laramie Treaty of 1851 in one article clearly stipulates that only one chief will be elected by the tribe to do national business. For example, nine chiefs were on hand to deal with during the Chippewa land Cession Treaty of 1837 creating an atmosphere that had some confusion and led to many questions to answer, forcing the negotiations to last much longer than the United States wanted. Stemming from the confusion came a great deal of obscure and unclear language that has led to much controversy and misunderstanding over the years since the Chippewa Treaty of 1837 was negotiated. The U.S. thus stipulated one chief to streamline the process and make the proceedings move along at a faster pace. But the faster pace can also be attributed to the fact that the treaties from 1851 on had the United States telling the Indians what it needed from them in land and rights to keep progress on track and dictated the type of lifestyle the Indian would now have to adopt.[2]

During the discussions for the Fort Laramie Treaty of 1851, the Great Sioux Reservation was established, and the Lakota only had one request, that no lines, or wagon trails and railroads, would cross their reservation, as they knew if any Americans crossed the Great Sioux Reservation they would not leave. The Lakota just wanted to be left alone and not be bothered so they could practice their traditional lifestyle. The United States simply told the Lakota that they would have to allow a few wagon trails to pass over some of the lower part of the reservation as the Lakota could and would not impede the growth of the California gold rush and not stand in the way of American progress. There were other important assimilation policies in this treaty as well. It was the first attempt to make the Lakota farmers. By having them take up farming the Lakota would now become a sedentary people and not nomadic. The 1851 Fort Laramie Treaty also had strict provisions on tribes going to war with each other and attacking white settlers passing thorough on their way to California. If any of the Lakota or other Plains tribes were caught off the reservations, went to war with each other, or attacked white settlers passing through they would either be killed or sent to prison at Fort Leavenworth Kansas. One provision of the Treaty of Fort Laramie 1851 that did allow a little of the old traditional ways of the Lakota and other Plains tribe prevail was that if a buffalo herd was large enough they were justified to wander off the reservations to hunt the buffalo, but as soon as they had enough kills they had to immediately return to the reservation.[3]

---

[1]Jeffery Ostler. *The Lakotas and the Black Hills: The Struggle for Sacred Ground* (New York: Penguin Group, 2004), 38–44.
[2]"Fort Laramie Treaty of 1851" Article 6.
[3]*Ibid.*, Articles 1–8.

The Dakota War of 1862

Meanwhile in southern Minnesota in 1851, a large land cession treaty was also signed between the state of Minnesota and the Dakota tribe, closely related to the Lakota. Little Crow, the major Dakota chief at this time in Minnesota, was reluctant to sign this treaty but eventually decided it was best to sign and get something for the tribe as the United States and the Territory of Minnesota would forcibly take it any way and the Dakota people would not receive anything for the land given up.[4]

The arrangement worked fairly well, but the Dakota people were in such a confined little tract of land, which made their reservation that they could not grow enough food or hunt for food. They were very dependent on the annuities and commodities given to them from the U.S. government. As time passed and with the outbreak of the American Civil War, the annuity payments were becoming later and later. Finally in 1862, the annuity payments were over two months late, and the Dakota people were starving. Little Crow and several other headmen went to see the Indian Agent at the St. Peters Agency, Andrew Myrick, at Fort Snelling. Here, little Crow explained the destitution of his people and the fact that many of his people were starving. Myrick simply answered, "If your people are starving, then let them eat grass." Little Crow told Myrick that he could not ensure the peace since when people become hungry they sometimes undertake acts of desperation.[5]

In August as the Dakota were becoming more desperate and hungry, four Dakota attacked a farm at Afton Minnesota and raided a U.S. government food storage center. Violence spread to all parts of Minnesota over the course of the next three weeks. After the disaster at the Second Battle of Bull Run, General Pope was released as commander of the Army of the Potomac, and was dispatched, along with all Minnesota units by President Abraham Lincoln, to go to Minnesota and end the war in Minnesota with the Dakota. Upon arriving in Minnesota, General Pope and the Minnesota military units were able to quite the war and drove all of the Dakota tribe out of Minnesota.[6]

The fact that the Dakota became refugees because of this war during the American Civil War is a greatly overlooked event in American history. The Dakota tribe was very split over whether to start attacking government food supplies or not. Dakota warriors that did carry out the acts of war against the United States and Minnesota were acting alone, but all Dakota paid the price of their actions. Many Dakota fled to the Great Sioux Reservation and were welcomed into the Lakota tribe, causing some crowding on the reservation. Other Dakota tribal members fled to Canada, where they were allowed to assimilate into the Assiniboine, Ojibwe, and Cree tribes of southwestern Ontario. The Dakota War of 1862 with the United States also ended the 130-year war with the Ojibwe tribe; the Dakota and Ojibwe had been waging war with each other over food sources. Only very few Dakota remained in Minnesota and settled in Indian communities that still exist today. Eventually, the Dakota that were chased out of Minnesota did filter back during the last half of the nineteenth century to live in the Dakota communities. The Ojibwe in Minnesota did not participate in this conflict and never left Minnesota and still have their reservations in Minnesota.[7]

Gold in Montana and the Fort Laramie Treaty of 1868

By 1863, more problems arose for the Lakota living on the Great Sioux Reservation. Gold had been discovered around the Montana town of Bozeman. The United States, at the request of mine owner John Bozeman, wanted a trail to be built and protected by the U.S. Army leaving the Oregon Trail at Fort Laramie going straight to his mines. By creating this trail, the miners could arrive in Bozeman much faster, cutting off one month of travel by the other route that would avoid traveling across the Great Sioux Reservation. The proposed Bozeman Trail would cut across the center of the Great Sioux Reservation, to the dismay of the Lakota.[8]

The U.S. government approved the trail and gave the army full authority over the making of the trail and providing protection from the Indian living in the area. The army built seven forts along the trail to provide

[4]Gary Clayton Anderson, *Little Crow: Spokesman for the Sioux* (St. Paul: The Minnesota Historical Society Press, 1986), 122.
[5]*Ibid.*, 122–123.
[6]*Ibid.*, 123–130.
[7]Charles Eastman. *Indian Boyhood*, (New York: McClure, Phillips, and Company, 1912), 245–264.
[8]PBS. *Custer's Last Stand*, 2012.

protection for miners traveling to the Bozeman mine. Encroachment on to the Great Sioux Reservation angered the Lakota, and this led what is commonly called Red Cloud's War. The war lasted from 1866 to 1868 and was an alliance between the Lakota, Arapaho, and Cheyenne tribes to try to stop further American expansion into their lands.[9]

Red Cloud's War directly led to the Fort Laramie Treaty of 1868. The 1868 Treaty of Fort Laramie was directed toward the Lakota. The United States needed to exhort more control over the Lakota and make them more dependent on the United States for food and other basic needs to live. The 1868 Treaty of Fort Laramie moved the boundaries of the Great Sioux Reservation further east, taking access to the great buffalo herds away from the Lakota. The boundaries were now better defined and the Lakota were told by the U.S. Army, who were the negotiators or dictators of the treaty, where the Lakota were to live, how they were to live or become farmers, and that if they were caught off the Great Sioux Reservation they would be taken to the military prison at Fort Leavenworth, Kansas. The provisions of the 1868 Fort Laramie Treaty emphasize that the Lakota become farmers. In Articles 6, 8, and 11 in the treaty, there are many benefits guaranteed to any Lakota man or head of a household to take up the plow. Double the number of acres from 160 to 320 acres for land ownership and all the equipment necessary to commence farming including the seeds. These were the first steps of the forced assimilation of the Lakota.[10]

The provisions of the 1868 Fort Laramie Treaty worked reasonably well until 1874. In 1870, the United States government added a new branch of the federal government called the United States Geological Service (USGS). These new scientists, or geologists, believed there were large deposits of gold and other precious minerals to be found in the Black Hills. The Lakota had been guaranteed possession of the Black Hills in both the 1851 and 1868 Treaties of Fort Laramie, and this now posed a problem for the U.S. government. In 1871, in a move to stop pushing Indian further west, the United States passed a law that simply stated that the United States was not making any more treaties with the Indian Nations. Treaty making was now officially over. Instead, the official policy of the United States was to assimilate Indians into mainstream American society, and those that did not assimilate were to be eradicated by starvation. But something had to be done now as the United States wanted possession of the Black Hills very badly.[11]

© Wollertz/Shutterstock, Inc.

---

[9]*Ibid.*
[10]"Fort Laramie Treaty of 1868." Articles 1–16.
[11]PBS. *Custer's Last Stand,* 2012.

President Ulysses S. Grant, William T. Sherman, and Philip Sheridan came up with a plan to force the Lakota to break the 1868 Treaty of Fort Laramie. They were going to send Lt. Colonel George Armstrong Custer into the Black Hills with a group of geologists and miners in an attempt to incite the Lakota to attack them inside the Great Sioux Reservation which would be a direct violation of the 1868 treaty, thus justifying the United States taking the Black Hills away from the Lakota. For the Lakota, the Black Hills were and still are a sacred space. In the center of the Black Hills is a place called Wind Cave, the place of origin and the place where the Lakota people emerged from the underworld and is a major part of their creation story. The Lakota have used the Black Hills as a place for reawaking their spirit, and a sacred place of spiritual healing. But as far as the United States was concerned, the gold in the Black Hills was far more important than and sacred space of an Indian tribe. In 1871, the era of treaty making came to an end. The United States said no more treaties were to be made or altered. Now it was time to civilize the central part of the United States and settle it. The United States needed more places to have the immigrants coming to it to settle, and the middle was where they were going.[12]

Sitting Bull, Little Big Horn, and the Taking Away of the Black Hills

Starting in 1874, Custer led many survey teams into the Black Hills and they did find large deposits of gold. In late 1874, Custer led some miners into the Black Hills and over the next two years several mining towns sprang up in the Black Hills on the Great Sioux Reservation, a direct violation of the United States's part of the 1868 Treaty of Fort Laramie. What the United States hoped to gain was that the Lakota would attack the min-

ers encroaching the Great Sioux Reservation and thus could take the Black Hills away from the Lakota. But the Lakota did not fall for that ploy and never attacked the miners, they complained to the Indian Agents living on the Great Sioux Reservation, but to no avail.[13]

In January 1876, President Grant, General Sherman, and General Sheridan sent out an order that all of the renegade bands of Lakota, Cheyenne, and other renegade bands of other tribes surrender themselves to the reservations or they will be hunted down by the U.S. Army and forced on to the reservations. Grant gave these renegade bands until January 26, 1876 to surrender. The deadline came and passed, and none of the renegade bands surrendered or confined themselves to the reservations.

By March of 1876, Grant, Sherman, and Sheridan decided that by the spring the army would be sent west to reinforce the troops in the Dakota Territory, and make an effort to track, primarily Sitting Bull and his renegade band of Lakota. They picked George A. Custer to be one of the primary leaders of this expedition to round up the renegade bands of Indians on the Plains and put them on the reservations.[14]

As the spring of 1876 approached, Sitting Bull sent out a call to all of the tribes on the Plains to come on

---

[12]*Ibid.*
[13]*Ibid.*
[14]*Ibid.*

out and enjoy this spring and summer as this will probably be the last time all of them could live the lifestyle of the old days. They could hunt buffalo and live the way the lived before the white man arrived in North America. Through May and June, thousands of Plains Indians arrived in eastern Montana Territory to live the lifestyle they loved and missed.[15]

In the middle of May, Custer and the men of the 7th Cavalry left Fort Lincoln in the Dakota Territory. They were part of a three-pronged attack designed by General Sheridan to push the Indians, once the attack commenced, into a trap from which they could not escape. The plan did not go as expected and instead Custer went out on his own and discovered the village of Indians that had come to join Sitting Bull for the summer at the place the Indians called the Greasy Grass and the whites called the Little Big Horn. There were nearly 12,000 Indians in that village, and Custer charged into battle believing the Indians would scatter and he would not be able to catch them. Instead the Indians charged Custer and his men with an overwhelming force that took only less than a half hour to totally annihilate Custer and his men. After the attack, Sitting Bull and his band left the encampment at the Greasy Grass and went to Canada. Even though Custer had been defeated and other parts of the task force to round up the renegade Indians had suffered some defeats and losses, all but Sitting Bull's band were forced onto the reservations.[16]

© Everett Historical/Shutterstock, Inc.

© Everett Historical/Shutterstock, Inc.

---

[15]*Ibid.*
[16]*Ibid.*

After the Battle of Little Big Horn, the United States started to look at a way to take away the Black Hills from the Lakota. In 1877, the United States said that Sitting Bull's renegade band, even though they were renegades and refused to observe and sign the Fort Laramie Treaty of 1868, violated the Fort Laramie Treaty of 1868 and took the Black Hills away from the Lakota. The United States made the Black Hills separate from the Great Sioux Reservation, and again the Lakota lost more land and were crowded onto smaller tracts of land. Sitting Bull and his renegade band of Lakota fled to Canada where the Royal Mounted Police told him they could stay in Canada as long they did not provoke any of the Canada tribes. In 1879, General Tarry went into Canada and told Sitting Bull that if he surrendered and succumbed to reservation life and surrendered his arms, the United States would allow him and his followers into the country without any consequences or prosecution. Sitting Bull declined the offer saying that he preferred Her Majesties land to the United States.[17]

The Boarding Schools

In 1875, Captain Richard Henry Pratt was placed in charge of seventy-two Apache prisoners that were to serve their prison sentences at Fort Marion Military Prison in St. Augustine, Florida. The Apache had been charged and found guilty of rape and murder of white settlers in the Arizona Territory. After a while, Pratt began to notice that the Apache prisoners seemed to learn better and faster away from their homes. Being separated from their people and native cultural surroundings seemed to make a great difference in the way they learned tasks and were learning English at a faster rate. Soon, Pratt started an outing program where the more advanced Apache in their education were placed in businesses in St. Augustine to earn some money and contribute to the local economy. The program was a big success as the Apache were well accepted by the St. Augustine community and the Apache both earned and spent money in the St. Augustine community.[18]

The success of Pratt's idea made think of a way to do this with many Indians. Pratt came up with the idea that maybe the United States should invest into a school or group of schools where Indian children would be housed and taught hundreds of miles away from their families and tribe. By separating the children from their families, tribe, and tribal culture, the children would learn English and "useful skills" faster to make them useful in mainstream American society. Pratt took his idea to Washington in 1878 with the knowledge that thirty of the seventy-two Apache went on to the Hampton Institute in Norfolk Virginia to further their education.[19]

Hampton Institute was an African American boarding school designed to help African Americans assimilate into mainstream American society and give the students a "useful skill" to be able to contribute to American society and be a useful person in the society. Pratt also had this idea in mind when he sent thirty of the Apache on to the Hampton Institute, and he was going to use the fact that it appeared that the Apache learned the American way better far away from home and separated from their family and tribe. As these students progressed at Hampton Institute, Pratt was able to approach Congress in early 1879 to try to attain funds to start, what he called, an Indian Industrial Boarding School, a place where the education provided would "Kill the Indian and save the man."[20]

Pratt's proposal included that the Indian children should be educated at least 500 miles from their reservation, family, and tribe. The greater the distance, the more effective the de-Indianizing education would be. The other half of the education was that the school was to be run in a military manner. Inserting a military drill and time system would regulate the Indian children and put them on a routine schedule, thus making it easier to educate them and teach them how to be white people. Presenting for the second time in two years, this time Congress granted Pratt some money and an old abandoned army post, to establish an Indian boarding school at Carlisle, Pennsylvania. The Carlisle Indian Industrial Boarding School was established and officially opened in October 1879.[21]

---

[17]*Ibid.*
[18]Mary A. Stout. *Native American Boarding Schools,* (Santa Barbara: Greenwood, 2012), 27–28.
[19]*Ibid.*
[20]Stout, 28–29.
[21]*Ibid.,* 29.

Congress did place some restrictions on Pratt's boarding school idea, such as he had to go and recruit his students, he had to obtain permission from parents of the students he recruited to go to Carlisle for five years, and the time period for each student was to be a maximum of five years at the school. The federal government did not want to put any more money in each student for more than five years. The U.S. government also told Pratt where his first students were to come from and that was the Pine Ridge and Rosebud Reservations in South Dakota. The Lakota was the tribe that resisted being placed on a reservation the longest and was the tribe that massacred Custer's 7th Calvary in 1876, and was considered one of the troublesome tribes. The U.S. government also could use the children as hostages if another Indian War broke out on the Plains. So the Lakota was the tribe the U.S. government wanted assimilated into mainstream American life first and as soon as possible. Pratt spent the summer of 1879 recruiting children for his school in Carlisle, and the target group was aged 4 to 12. Most educators and psychologists in 1879 believed that ages 4 to 12 was the time in every child's life where they learned the most and when a child was most impressionable to ideas. By the fall of 1879, Pratt had met the government's goal and quota for him to proceed with the experiment of the Indian Industrial Boarding School of sixty-six children. The parents and grandparents of the first sixty-six children for Pratt's school were brought to the train station and all said goodbye, wondering if they would ever see each other again. The 900-mile journey to Carlisle, Pennsylvania, was especially hard on the four- to six-year-olds as they knew no one and at this tender age was very difficult to be away from their parents.[22]

After arriving at Carlisle, the homesickness and fear only became magnified as the first thing that happened to each student was a haircut. To Indians and especially Indian children, having their hair cut for no reason is very traumatic. Indians only cut their hair when in mourning for the loss of a family member or after having failed very badly in life. In the case of failure, the hair is cut to single the person out to every member of the tribe. These children were confused as to why their hair was cut and they had to wear a uniform instead of their traditional clothes. Their traditional clothes were taken to the back of the boarding school and burned. Being treated in this manner only intensified the homesickness and made many Indian children feel ashamed of themselves for really no reason. The United States and Pratt were very insensitive to the culture and life of the Indian children. During the Indian boarding schools existence, from 1879 to 1998, 500 Indian boarding schools came into existence. Three schools remain today, but they are in a different capacity today as they are Native American colleges today and run by Native Americans. The schools are the Institute of American Indian Art, in Santa Fe, New Mexico, formally the Santa Fe Industrial Indian School, opened in 1890; The Haskell Indian Nations University, formally the United States Indian Industrial Training School, Lawrence, Kansas, opened in 1884; and Sherman Institute, formally the Riverside Indian School, Riverside, California, opened in 1892. Today, these schools are three of the best Indian schools offering the best in Indian cultural education and are run by Native Americans.[23]

The reason the hair was cut and all of the children had to wear uniforms that made them look all alike was to make them look like white children. Now the first part of the plan to assimilate Indian children into white culture was done. Next, the children would start military drill and eat a diet of American food and not the traditional foods they were accustomed to. The drills were intended to force the Indian children into regular routine of drill, eat a meal at a certain time, and go to classes to learn a useful vocation. The classes to learn a useful vocation were considered extremely important as this was to give the Indian children a skill than would let them become a useful member of American society. At this time, the Indian children cannot be called useful citizens as Indians do not have American citizenship. They will not receive citizenship until 1924. Being treated in the way only made the Indian children more homesick and scared.[24]

There was one other aspect of the boarding schools that was very cruel and that was the children could only speak English. Pratt believed that taking away the native language of the children was the key to make them forget their culture. If they were caught speaking their native languages, they were severely punished. Usually the punishment was a severe beating and/or washing the child's mouth out with soap. There were several recorded cases where a child choked to death while having their mouth washed out with soap. The idea of

---

[22]*Ibid.*, 29–30.
[23]*Ibid.*, 30–31.
[24]*Ibid.*, 31–36.

the schools was to kill Indian culture, and one of the main ways to do this was to take and kill Native American languages. Over time, the boarding schools were very effective in nearly destroying Native American languages and killing the culture. Children attending these schools were not supposed to return home. They were to, after graduating from the school, assimilate into mainstream American society, contributing to American society utilizing the useful skill they had learned in school. The children were to have no recollection of their culture, home, family, and language. They were to know English only and would be able to work for white Americans. As for the family that was left on the reservations, they were to die off. Since no children were left on the reservation to carry on the traditions, Indian culture, cultural practices, and language would die off and that would be the end of the "Indian Problem" as many Americans viewed Indians as a problem. Indians would become a people of the past and would be considered extinct.[25]

There was another very bad side to these schools, and that was the living conditions. Because most of the schools were old military buildings that were abandoned, they were in disrepair and were very cold and damp places to live. The Indian children were crowded into very small spaces, which allowed diseases to spread very quickly. By far, tuberculosis was the disease that was the leading cause of death among the students that attended the boarding schools. Following tuberculosis were influenza, measles, smallpox, trachoma, and suicide as the common causes of illness and death. Trachoma was an eye disease, and though fatal in extreme cases, this disease generally caused blindness if left untreated. In several cases in the first decade of the twentieth century, medical science had developed a surgical procedure that doctors believed would alleviate the disease. The boarding schools opened up their doors and allowed doctors to perform the new procedure on the Indian children that were suffering from the effects of trachoma. Many of the doctors and school officials viewed preforming this procedure on the Indian children as good as they felt that they are just Indians and that even if they lose their sight it is no real big deal. Unfortunately, this was the attitude that existed in mainstream American society at this time in history toward Indians.[26]

Many Indian children died while attending these schools, and unfortunately about half of these deaths were suicides. The pressure, culture shock, and homesickness caused by being separated from their families was just too much for many of the Indian students. Sadly, of all of the deaths that occurred in these schools, less than 2 percent of the children's bodies were returned their homes for a proper tribal burial. In fact, only about 2 percent of the Indian families that had children attending these schools ever knew what happened to their children if they did not come home from the school after five years. In the cemetery located on the grounds of the Carlisle Indian Industrial School, almost all of the graves are marked as Unknown Indian Child; so they never went home and the family back home never knew what happed to their child. So it was not only the children that missed their families, the families too missed their children and were deeply saddened and scared as many children never came home. The last time many families saw their children was at the train station or when U.S. Indian Agents came to their homes to forcibly remove the children from their families. Some children did return home only to be rejected by their families, causing at least three generations of Indian children to have a cultural void and loss of Native American identity. The problem still exists today and is being dealt with, but the scars of the boarding school system are still felt today, coupled with the loss and near extinction of all Native American languages. The boarding schools were about 90 percent effective in eliminating Indian culture and language, but not fully successful, and the Indians still exist today are reclaiming their cultural ways. The boarding school era was a very dark era in the long relations between the Americans and the Native Americans. In 1934, armed with the results of the Meriam Report and with the Indian Reorganization Act of 1934, the boarding school system was slowly phased out, with the last school closing—St. Catherine's in Santa Fe New Mexico in 1998.[27]

One unintended consequence of the failure of government-run Indian Industrial Boarding Schools was they brought Indian children from many tribes together and taught them English. What the schools and Pratt took a great deal of pride—teaching the Indian children English and using this as a way to take their culture away from the Indian children—turned out to be the avenue for the beginnings of Indian resistance

---

[25]*Ibid.*, 35–36.

[26]*Ibid.*, 40–42.

[27]*Ibid.*, 42–44.

movements. As these Indian children began to know and communicate with each other, something began to happen. They began to exchange boarding school experiences and share their cultures with each other. Out of this, by 1911, several boarding school graduates came together to form The Society of American Indians that was a lobby and pressure group of American Indians fighting for Indian rights, and they began pressuring the U.S. government to make changes to Federal Indian Policy and close the government-run Indian Industrial Boarding Schools.

Gertrude Bonnin became one of the major leaders of this movement. She became a teacher and taught at Carlisle for two years and was appalled at what she saw. Bonnin had a terrible experience at the Whites Institute of Indian Manual Labor School in Wabash, Indiana. The cutting of her hair was devastating to her, and after graduating from the school she went home to become an outcast. Her mother had a difficult time communicating with her, and in many ways viewed her daughter as dead. Bonnin left the reservation never to return and went on to become an educator graduating from Earlham College in Richmond, Indiana. She became an educator at Carlisle for two years, and there began her quest to close the boarding schools. She was distraught over the way the Indian children were treated by the white teachers and staff. Many of the colleagues were alcoholics or opium addicts. She did not like seeing the sexual harassment of the Indian girls by male teaches. While at Carlisle, Bonnin wrote five articles that appeared in both the *Atlantic Monthly* and *Harper's Bazaar,* both very popular magazines of the early twentieth century that middle-class American read. She brought attention and awareness to the issue of the boarding schools. Here began the movement of progressive Americans to begin to question Federal Indian Policy toward American Indians, and they began to pressure the federal government to make changes. Bonnin dedicated the rest of her life for the betterment of her people. This happened because the United States believed it was killing Indian culture by forcing the Indian children to speak English, but instead it gave the Indian children a way to communicate with each other and begin to work together to force change.[28]

The Dawes Allotment Act of 1887

Massachusetts U.S. Senator Henry Dawes was one of many people during the last half of the nineteenth century who was very concerned about the welfare of the Indians. Over the previous 150 years, the Indians had been pushed farther and farther west, and in 1871 there was to be no more treaties made or renegotiated. Because Indians seemed helpless against the expansion of the United States, a group formed called the *Friends of the Indian,* and Dawes was one of the leaders of this group. The Indians were steadily losing land in one way or another. Either they were being encroached on by miners that were illegally entering reservation land or they were having the land taken away by the U.S. government through provoked treaty infringements.

Senator Dawes would become a big influence on Indians and their land holding through the end of the nineteenth century and the early twentieth century. In 1887, Dawes came up with an idea that he believed would really help the Indians out and help the students returning from the boarding schools. The Dawes Allotment Act was passed in 1887, and its intention was to force the tribal members take possession of the land and become farmers. It worked like this: the head of a household was to receive 160 acres, a single person over eighteen and orphans were to receive 80 acres, a single persons under eighteen were to receive 40 acres. Two things were to happen from the Dawes Allotment Act. One, Indians were taking ownership of individual parcels of land and becoming farmers, with the excess land going up for sale and being sold to the U.S. government with that land in turn being resold to white settlers, who were mainly farmers. Two, this was a way to break up tribalism that the Indians clung to very hard. The United States was trying to make Indians see the American way that land holdings were an individual right and that land was not something to be viewed a community holding, that the land belonged to the tribe as a whole, but something each person owned individually. By breaking up the reservations or putting white settlers between tribal members would make the Indians become individual land owners. But in reality, the Dawes Allotment Act only made the reservations look like checkerboards.[29]

---

[28]*Ibid.,* 36–37.

[29]Wilcomb E. Washburn. *The Assault on Indian Tribalism,* (Malabar: Charles E Krieger Publishing Company, 1986), 3–31.

The Dawes Allotment Act also was to work in conjunction with the boarding school system in helping the young Indians graduating from these schools to better use the land or be able to sell the land to white land speculators, giving the young Indians money to help them either start a business or some other endeavor. It did not work out that way as many of the students came back to the reservations and were given land on the opposite side of the reservation so as to be separated from their families, and they then refused to sell their land to white speculators. But the Dawes Allotment Act did become just another way for the United States to take away more land from the Indians. The Federal Land Trust also was set up at this time and is controversial. The federal government bought land from the Indians instead of giving them the money directly, and this was placed in a trust fund for the benefit of the tribes. This fund has many issues surrounding it in 1887, and even today nobody knows how much money is in the fund and nobody can audit the books or look at the book. So, many Indian believe there is no money in the fund and that they have lost not only more land because of the Dawes Allotment Act but all of the money owed to the tribes by the United States as well. During the time that the Dawes Allotment Act was in effect, Indians lost over 70 percent of the land holdings they had. By 1934 when the Dawes Allotment Act was repealed, the Indians went from, in 1492, holding all of the land in the continental United States to, in 1934, only holding 2 percent of the land.[30]

As the 1880s were arriving, many tribes in the west were becoming desperate. They had seen all of their land holdings diminish, their children were being taken away from them, they no longer could hunt buffalo as their ancestors had, and the buffalo were also disappearing. The buffalo was a sacred thing in Native American religion. One tribe in particular was beginning to feel very desperate, and that tribe was the Lakota. The Lakota watched their children be dragged off to the boarding schools, and the ones that did return were not recognizable. They watched helplessly as their land was slowly being taken away. They watched as one of their religious symbols was beginning to rapidly disappear, the buffalo. The Lakota and other tribes in the west were asking **Wonka Tonka** (the Lakota name for God) "Why are you letting this happen to us." Through the 1860s and 1870s, something was developing that would give the Lakota and other tribes some hope: **The Ghost Dance Religion.**[31]

The Ghost Dance Religion

During a soul renewal ceremony called the Sundance in the Great Basin in southern Utah in the 1870s to 1880s, a Paiute Indian named Wovoka passed out and had a dream. In the dream, Wovoka said the sky opened up and all of the departed ancestors of the Indian people returned and with them the buffalo returned to the Plains as in the old days before the whites had arrived. The ancestors told Wovoka that the Indian people were to treat each other well and help each other. They were to forsake the ways of the whites and to leave alcohol along, and stop drinking. They needed to go back to the traditional ways and leave the ways of the whites behind. The Lakota were to do this dance and then the buffalo would return, the Indians would again rule the Plains and the white man would disappear. The spirits then taught Wovoka the Ghost Dance.[32]

The message given to Wovoka was given before by the Prophet in 1806, so this message resurfaced saying the Indian people needed to not adopt the ways of the whites but to practice their traditional culture. The Indians now had something to believe in, and the Ghost Dance began to spread very quickly all over the west. By 1880s, the Lakota became very curious about the Ghost Dance and sent Kicking Bear to the Great Basin to see what the dance was all about.[33]

At the same time Kicking Bear was heading west, Sitting Bull returned to the Standing Rock reservation and agency in North Dakota. Sitting Bull and his renegade band had been living in Canada since Little Big Horn had occurred in 1876. The Canadian government had told Sitting Bull that as long as his people behaved and did not stir up any trouble among the Canadian Indian tribes they could live in Canada. From 1876 to 1883, several of Sitting Bull's band left Canada and went to live on the reservation because they were

---

[30]*Ibid.*, 3–31.
[31]Philip Burnham. *Song of Dewy Beard: Last Survivor of Little Big Horn* (Lincoln: University of Nebraska Press, 2014). 57–87.
[32]*Ibid.*
[33]*Ibid.*

missing their families. But in 1883, the Canadian government paid Sitting Bull a visit telling him to settle down or turn over the young men of his band that had been stealing horses form neighboring tribes, or leave Canada. Sitting Bull took care of the young men that had been stealing the horses and dealt with them in the Lakota way. Sitting Bull also returned the stolen horses and decided it was time for his band to go back to the United States to the reservation. In the spring of 1883, Sitting Bull arrived at the Standing Rock Agency on the Standing Rock Reservation and placed his rifle on the desk of the Indian Agent, saying "I want to be known in history as the last Indian to surrender his gun." Sitting Bull and his band then proceeded to settle on the Stand Rock Reservation.[34]

By late summer of 1883, Kicking Bear returned from the Great Basin and told and taught many Lakota about the Ghost Dance. Bigfoot, a young and upcoming Lakota chief, was really enthusiastic about the Ghost Dance and encouraged all of his band to learn the Ghost Dance as this may be the miracle they had been looking for to end the nightmare of the last 400 years. Kicking Bear went to Sitting Bull, and Sitting Bull was not fully convinced that the Ghost Dance would help but he said that if any of his band wanted to learn the Ghost Dance they should do so. Sitting Bull viewed the Ghost Dance as a way to at least give his people some hope in these trying times for the Lakota. They really had nothing to lose.[35]

© Reid Dalland/Shutterstock, Inc.

As time went by and more and more Lakota began to practice the Ghost Dance, the Indian Agents on the Lakota reservations and the U.S. government became very nervous over the Ghost Dance and first banned all Native American religious practices and dances. By November 1890, as many as 10,000 Lakota were hiding out in the Black Hills practicing the Ghost Dance and making the Indian Agent at Standing Rock and the Agent at Pine Ridge extremely nervous and asking for more Army soldiers. The U.S. government responded to the requests for more troops and sent in 5,000 more troops including the 7th Cavalry, Custer's old unit that was massacred at the Little Big Horn, and many of the Lakota on both Standing Rock and Pine Ridge Reservations had participated in the massacre at the Little Big Horn in 1876; this fact only added more tension to an already very tense situation.[36]

Wounded Knee 1890

The situation for the Indian Agents by December 1890 was becoming desperate because it was rumored that Sitting Bull was about to join the Ghost Dancers. Sitting Bull was still a strong leader among the Lakota, and

---

[34]HBO Films, *Bury My Heart at Wounded Knee*, 2007.
[35]Burnham, 57–87.
[36]*Ibid.*

the Indian Agents feared with the large number of Lakota in the area another massacre like Little Big Horn could happen again at either Pine Ridge or Standing Rock Reservations.[37]

The Indian Agent on December 13, 1890 ordered the Indian police force to go to Standing Rock Reservation and arrest Sitting Bull and bring him in. Fear and nervousness was everywhere on the reservations in the Dakota Territory at this time. Early in the morning on December 13, 1890, forty-three Indian police officers arrived at Sitting Bull's cabin and forcibly entered the cabin. The officers brought Sitting Bull to the door of the cabin where they were met by several of Sitting Bull's band. After an exchange of words, a shot was fired and one officer was wounded and another shot was fired that hit Sitting Bull in the head, killing him instantly. Sitting Bull was now dead, the Lakota had now lost their inspirational leader. The last prophecy, or vision of Sitting Bull had now came true, that he would be killed by his own people. Sitting Bull had several visons about Little Big Horn, and they were very accurate and his last vision was also very accurate as to what his fate was to be.[38]

Sitting Bull's band of followers were now lost. After Sitting Bull's death, the Ghost Dance was not producing the desired results. Sitting Bull's band decided to find and join Bigfoot's band and see what would happen. Upon joining Bigfoot's band, the followers of Sitting Bull and Bigfoot's band were beginning to feel very downtrodden and desperate. Bigfoot decided that since the Ghost Dance did not seem to deliver the magic promised, maybe it was time for the Ghost Dancers to go to the Pine Ridge Agency to surrender and negotiate a settlement and resign to reservation life. Bigfoot started the trek to Pine Ridge Reservation.[39]

At the same time, General Nelson Miles, who Washington sent to administer to the problem of the Ghost Dance on the Plains, dispatched Colonel Forsythe and the 7th Cavalry, Custer's old unit from the Little Big Horn, to find and intercept Bigfoot's band of Ghost Dancers before they stirred up any trouble. On the evening of December 28, 1890, Forsythe found and confronted Bigfoot's band and the remaining part of Sitting Bull's band at Wounded Knee Creek. Most of the Indians were very hungry and several were sick, including Bigfoot, who had a severe case of pneumonia. The soldiers gave the Indians food for the night and everyone made camp. But during the night, the soldiers were ordered to set up four Hotchkiss guns around the Indian encampment.[40]

Mid-morning on December 29, 1890, all of the men in the Indian camp were ordered out to the center of the encampment to be disarmed. Forsythe had not really understood what Bigfoot's intention was at this point, wanting to surrender to the Indian Agent at the Pine Ridge Indian Agency. Forsythe believed that Bigfoot was moving his band to group with other Ghost Dancers and treated the Indians accordingly. The Indian men were ordered to give up their weapons and a few rifles were surrendered. Soldiers began to search the tipis of the Lakota for weapons, and did find a few knives and a couple of guns in the tipis.[41]

Most of the Lakota really believed in the Ghost Dance and since then had created special Ghost Dance shirts. The Medicine Men told them that these shirts were bullet proof. The bullets of the white men would not penetrate the shirts and as long as the Lakota people wore these shirts they would be safe. There was a Medicine Man that was performing the Ghost Dance on a small hill behind the Indian encampment. At the same time, the soldiers had only one Lakota man to convince to turn his rifle. It turns out this Lakota man was deaf and did not understand that the soldiers wanted him to give up his rifle and a struggle began to disarm the deaf man. At the same time the struggle began, the Lakota Medicine Man preforming the Ghost Dance on the hill behind the encampment threw some dirt in the air at the same time the rifle of the deaf Lakota man went off, and all hell broke loose after that shot. The U.S. army opened up on 300 unarmed Lakota men, women, and children with ling range rifles and the four Hotchkiss guns. These guns were small cannons that fired exploding shells, and the fire was directed into the tipis, killing and wounding many women and children. In the end 300 Lakota were dead, and over half were women and children.[42]

---

[37]*Ibid.*
[38]*Ibid.*
[39]*Ibid.*
[40]*Ibid.*
[41]*Ibid.*
[42]*Ibid.*

On the evening of December 29, 1890, a major blizzard came and the dead bodies of the Lakota were left in the snow. Colonel Forsythe and his 7th Cavalry had to quell uprisings on the Pine Ridge Reservation over the next three days until the last 4,000 Ghost Dancers surrendered. Finally on January 2, 1891, a burial crew arrived to bury the 300 Lakota that were killed on December 29, 1890. The Lakota were buried in a mass grave next to Wounded Knee Creek, on the Pine Ridge Reservation. All armed Indian resistance on the Plains and everywhere to the United States ended with the Wounded Knee Massacre of 1890. The massacre left a deep scar among not only the Lakota, but all Indian people in the United States. Indian and white relations all revolve around this one incident and will never be forgotten by not just the Lakota but all Indian people. It is still a focal point and stumbling block to Indian and U.S. government relations and Indian and white relations today.[43]

Works Cited

Burnham, Philip. *Song of Dewy Beard: Last Survivor of Little Big Horn,* Lincoln: University of Nebraska Press, 2014.

Clayton, Anderson Gary. *Little Crow: Spokesman for the Sioux,* St. Paul: The Minnesota Historical Society Press, 1986.

Eastman, Charles. *Indian Boyhood,* New York: McClure, Phillips, and Company, 1912.

HBO Films. *Bury My Heart at Wounded Knee,* 2007.

Ostler, Jeffery. *The Lakota and the Black Hills: The Struggle for Sacred Ground,* New York: Penguin Books, 2010.

PBS. Video *Custer's Last Stand,* 2012.

Stout, Mary A. *Native American Boarding Schools,* Santa Barbara: Greenwood, 2012.

United States. *Treaty of Fort Laramie* September 17, 1851. Cankú Lúta (Red Road, Inc.) (accessed February 25, 2015).

United States. *Treaty of Fort Laramie 1868* April 29, 1868. www.ourdocuments.gov (accessed February 25, 2015).

Washburn, Wilcomb E. *The Assault on Indian Tribalism,* Malabar: Robert E. Krieger Publishing, 1986.

---

[43] *Ibid.*

Chapter 8

Indian Renewal and Cultural Revitalization

The Progressive Era

In the decade after Wounded Knee in 1890, things did not get any better for the Lakota or, for that fact, any American Indian tribe in the United States. When the U.S. Census of 1900 came out, many white people became concerned. There were only 237,196 Native Americans left in the United States. Not only was the number of Native Americans low, but the number of buffalo was also low, with only 250,000 buffalo left on the Plains. The policy of eradication that the United States adopted in the last half of the nineteenth century had been effective—take the food supply away from the Indians by hunting the buffalo into extinction—but in 1900 there were still Native Americans around.[1]

A new group of people were materializing in the United States, and they were called the Progressives. The Progressives saw the low numbers of both the buffalo and Native Americans and became concerned. They started a movement called "Save the Indian" and at the same time moved to save the buffalo from extinction as well. The Progressives gained strength in 1901 when Theodore Roosevelt became president of the United States after President William McKinley was assassinated. Roosevelt had lived and visited the west over the last twenty years of the nineteenth century and believed the land, buffalo, and Native Americans needed to be saved. Progressive people had many good intentions, but their ideas for saving the Indians was misguided and only opened the opportunity to create the Indian stereotype that exists today.

The Progressives started collecting as many Indian artifacts, made sound recordings of Indian songs and Indian voices in general. Others, like Edward Curtiss, went to primarily the southwestern United States and took as many photographs as he could of the Indians living there before they disappeared. Others such as Mable Dodge Lohan moved to the Santa Fe area from New York City and began to collect Pueblo art works, consisting of both watercolor paintings and Pueblo pottery. Pueblo pottery is very valuable today and some of the vessels are worth hundreds of thousands of dollars, depending on who made them, an example would be Maria Martinez.[2]

Dodge and other eastern seaboard people also moved to the Santa Fe area, creating the "Santa Fe intellectual club," and worked with the Pueblo Indians often on issues and preservation of their culture. These "intellectuals" did do some good in the line of promoting Pueblo art and brought attention to the Pueblos and their culture. Many women at this time came to the Santa Fe area to learn about Pueblo feminism and sexuality and worked to incorporate those values into mainstream American culture during the Progressive Era. Along with all of the wealthy New Yorkers moving to the Santa Fe area, many archeologists and anthropologists also came southwest to preserve the Pueblo culture that they were sure was going to disappear.[3]

---

[1]Michael McGerr. *A Fierce Discontent: The Rise and Fall or the Progressive Movement In America* (New York: Oxford University Press, 2003), 202–203.
[2]*Ibid.*, 242–245.
[3]*Ibid.*

But Indians did not disappear, and they were beginning their resistance in a different way without guns. With the unexpected help of the Progressives in education and other reforms that were put in place between 1900 and 1920, Indians began to move forward into a better life. It may not look like it on the surface, because this is the peak time of the government-run boarding school system with thirty-four schools being directly run by the U.S. government and over 500 being run by the Catholic Church and funded by the U.S. government, and this was thus a dark time for many Indian children and parents. But many of the these children were taking advantage of learning English, a common language to communicate with each other, to begin forming pressure groups to begin to exert pressure on the United States to enact a change in Federal Indian policy. Very educated Indians such as Charles Eastman, Carlos Montezuma, and Gertrude Bonnin came together to form a very important group that was the very first from of organized Indian resistance to American Colonialism—The Society of American Indians (SAI).[4]

The Society of American Indians

Coming from the boarding school system and entering American higher education, Charles Eastman and Carlos Montezuma became medical doctors and began a life dedicated to help improve the conditions of American Indians. Both men were the result of what Progressives believed Indians could do through Progressive education and that was blend the best of both cultures and become better people because of the blending of the best qualities of both cultures, American and American Indian cultures. Eastman became the reservation physician for the Pine Ridge Reservation in South Dakota and was the doctor on call when the Wounded Knee Massacre occurred on December 29, 1890. The cruel act performed by the U.S. 7th Cavalry had an impact on Eastman. He began to question what was really going on with both cultures and came to believe that instead of bring out the best in both cultures the Americans only intention was to keep colonizing Indians and to try to annihilate the Indian race. Eastman by 1900 started to go back to his Dakota ways and began to combine Dakota and American ways to help him keep his Dakota heritage alive and to have enough knowledge of the American ways to help him navigate his way in the new world of the dominate American culture to be able to function in that culture, but keep his Dakota roots alive within him.[5]

Many of the same circumstances were occurring to Montezuma in the American southwest. After Carlos Montezuma graduated from the University of Illinois in 1884, he worked at the Carlisle Indian School until 1900 when he moved to Chicago to set up a private medical practice. In 1903, "Pop" Warner, the football coach for Carlisle asked Montezuma to accompany the Carlisle football team to Arizona and the southwest as the team physician. Montezuma accepted the offer and upon arriving in Arizona, a place Montezuma had not visited since he left the area at age 5, during his boyhood, and appalled at the conditions his people, the Apache Tribe, were expected to live in through the U.S. reservation system. Montezuma finished the football tour with Coach Werner and the Carlisle team and returned in 1903 to the reservations in his homeland, Arizona and the American southwest, to try to help his people the Apache. As the physician for several reservations, Montezuma became extremely frustrated by the lack of medical equipment and other medicines need to treat simple aliments. The fact that the federal government was very slow at responding to the needs of the Apache people began to make Montezuma very angry and upset. He began to think as to how he could best help his people, and Indians in general, in the United States. [6]

In 1905, Montezuma made national headlines in the United States by starting the first organization dedicated to help Indians in the United States and work for public knowledge of the conditions on reservations and the evils of the boarding school system. From this point on, Montezuma become an activist on behalf of all Indian people in the United States. By 1911, the organization became more organized and began to attract other higher educated Indians and what was called in the Progressive Era "Middle Class Indians." Indians

---

[4]John W. Larner, Jr., Ed. *The Papers of the Society of American Indians* parts 1 and 2 Wilmington DE: Scholarly Resources, 1987. Microfilm.
[5]*Ibid.*
[6]Carlos Montezuma. Gale Encyclopedia of Biography, Answers.com. http://answers.com/topic/montezuma-carlos (accessed January 15, 2014).

like Luther Standing Bear, who had completed the boarding school education and either returned to the reservation as he did or had ventured into the mainstream American culture and created a business or were preforming an occupation that was useful to American society were considered "Middle Class Indians."[7]

On October 12, 1911 at The Ohio State University in Columbus, Ohio, The SAI held its first convention. The date and location of the convention was internally chosen as a symbolic protest over Columbus Day. Back in those days, Columbus Day was always October 12, because that was the actual day according to Christopher Columbus's diary he and his men sighted land after ninety days at sea. He and his men went ashore and encountered the Native American people. In those days, Columbus Day was not arranged to create a federal holiday for government works, it was celebrated on whatever day of the week October 12 fell, it did not matter if it fell on a Wednesday or a Monday; it was celebrated on the day of the week it fell. Montezuma and Eastman wanted the first convention of SAI to open on Columbus Day and in Columbus to draw attention to, first, the convention and, second, that American Indians really do not believe that Columbus's coming to the Americas was a great event in the history of American Indians. This was because, simply put, the lifestyles of Indian people were changed forever and some tribe disappeared because of Columbus. SAI really wanted to state the felling of all Indians everywhere in the Americas that Columbus first gave them the name Indians because he was not accurately aware of where he actually was, he thought he was in the East Indies and hence he named the people he found Indians. Second, Montezuma and other members of SAI really believed that American needed to know how Indians really felt about Columbus as a real negative in their history and believed the day should be called Indian Day to honor how their live and history was forever changed by Columbus coming to the Americas. Over the last two to three years, this particular issues has surfaced again with many Native American populations all over the United States demanding the name of Columbus Day be changed to Indigenous Day to celebrate how the Indian's lives were changed and to celebrate the culture and tribes that have been lost over the last 500+ years since Columbus arrive in the Americas.[8]

In 1916, Gertrude Bonnin joined the SAI and became the most vocal of all of the members nationwide. She was an advocate to end the government-run boarding schools and began a strong movement to end the practice. We remember Bonnin from the chapter on the boarding schools and her traumatic experience at White's Institute of Indian Manual Labor, in Wabash, Indiana. Her return home was just as traumatic as her mother did not recognize her and rejected Bonnin as her daughter. Since the time Bonnin left the Yankton Reservation in South Dakota, she dedicated her life to the end of the institution of boarding schools.[9]

While Bonnin was involved with the SAI, she became very outspoken on the boarding school issue and general living conditions on reservations. Bonnin brought a lot of attention to SAI and between 1916 and 1925, and she wrote several articles denouncing the boarding schools system that were published in the *Atlantic Monthly and Harper's Bazaar*. She brought to the forefront the problems that Indians had with the boarding schools system, the cruelty of the institutions, and how the boarding school system was destroying Indian culture and tearing Indian families apart. Many Americans did begin to respond to the issues the Indians were facing as presented through the articles Bonnin wrote.[10]

Bonnin believed that the SAI was not radical enough for her and she left the organization in 1923 and started her own pressure group called the Congress of American Indians, and that group still exists today. Bonnin became very vocal on Indian rights and the problem of broken treaties and other issues. She was the first to really point out how treaty rights were being violated and how Indians were being treated in general.[11]

Bonnin was not the only person in the United States that was beginning to question what was wrong with Federal Indian Policy. President Calvin Coolidge also was beginning to question what was going in with Federal Indian Policy. Coolidge had read Bonnin's articles and wanted to know where all of the federal money was going to on reservations, as it seemed no matter how much money was spent by the U.S. government, the living conditions of the Indians seemed to just get worse. In 1926, President Coolidge commissioned Lewis

---

[7] *Ibid.*
[8] Larner, parts 1 and 2.
[9] Mary A. Stout, *Native American Boarding Schools* (Santa Barbara: Greenwood, 2012), 144–146.
[10] *Ibid.*, 144–146.
[11] *Ibid.*

Meriam to form a commission and investigate how Federal Indian Policy was functioning on the reservations and the effects of said policy on the everyday lives of Indian people. One of the first Meriam asked to serve on the Meriam Commission was Gertrude Bonnin. Because she had been so vocal about Federal Indian Policy and the boarding school system, she was asked to serve not only by Meriam but also by President Coolidge, who wanted to know what Bonnin thought as well.[12]

The Meriam Report

Meriam for the next two years went to every reservation in the United States. They looked at how federal money was spent, who was overseeing the spending, and the general living conditions on each reservation. The Meriam Commission concluded in 1928 and issued its report in November 1928. To many Americans, the findings were very surprising and disturbing.

The Meriam Report concluded that all Indians living on the reservations were in very poor health and were malnourished. The education systems both on and off the reservations were total failures, with most of the money going toward administration and not educating young Indians. All Indians on average upon completing both on and off reservations schooling only had the a 4th grade education, thus making it impossible to function in mainstream American life. The report concluded that a complete overhaul of the Federal Indian Policy was needed, and needed as soon as possible. The report recommended that the first priorities and needs of the American Indians was that they needed better food and nutrition and better access to health care to become more healthy which would greatly help in the education of the young. The report also concluded that Indians themselves needed to have more control over the education of their children and that the government-run boarding school system should be phased out. Not only should tribes have more control of their children's education, the tribes needed to have more governmental control over themselves. In other words, the tribes should have their own tribal governments to administer to their people and have more control of their destinies. American Indians were to be allowed to have tribal sovereignty, something that was to be guaranteed to them from the beginning. Here is the beginning of the way tribes look today. The Meriam Report was released at the very end of President Coolidge's tenure as President of the United States, and too late for him to take action on the Meriam Report's findings and recommendations. When Herbert Hoover became the next President of the United States, he did implement some of the recommendations of the Meriam report, but October 29, 1929 changed Hoover's course of action on implementing the Meriam Report's findings and recommendations. As America entered into the Great Depression, changes to Federal Indian Policy would have to be placed on the back burner. It would take a change of Presidential administrations and recovery from the Great Depression to instill change on Indian Reservations and Federal Indian Policy, tribal sovereignty, and Indian education.[13]

The Great Depression and the Indian New Deal

When Franklin D. Roosevelt became President of the United States in 1933, nobody knew what to expect, especially on the Indian Reservations. After Roosevelt came into office, he started to appoint cabinet members to his administration. One of those members was John Collier, who became the Commissioner of Indian Affairs. Collier's appointment is very important as he was the man that initiated sweeping change to Federal Indian Policy.

Roosevelt chose Collier because of his knowledge of Indians, especially the tribes in the southwest, the Navajo, Pueblo, and Hopi tribes. Looking at Collier's background before becoming Commissioner of Indian Affairs reveals an interesting career in social work, public service, and service to the tribes in the American southwest. Collier started his social work career in 1890 at Ellis Island in New York City. His job was helping and directing immigrants arriving from Central Europe to locations in the mid-west to settle. After thirty

---

[12]*Ibid.*

[13]*The Meriam Report: The Problem of Indian Administration,* National Indian Law Library. https://narf.org/nill/resources/meriam.html (accessed October 10, 2014).

years in this position, Collier contracted tuberculosis by 1920 and moved to northern New Mexico where the weather was drier and warmer, which allowed him to better deal with the disease. In northern New Mexico, Collier lived with and became very attached to the Pueblo Indians and became a member of the Santa Fe Intellectual Club. Collier learned many aspects of Pueblo culture and religion and became convinced that the only salvation for the white race was to adopt many parts of the Pueblo culture and incorporate it into the better parts of the white culture to save it. Looking at Collier's past makes it easier to understand why he made such radical changes to Federal Indian Policy.[14]

By 1934, Collier had drafted the Indian Reorganization Act, or IRA for short, calling for the end of the government-run boarding school system, the repeal of the disastrous Dawes Allotment Act of 1887 to stop the taking of reservation land from the Indians, and to let tribes create their sovereign governments to control their own destinies. While the IRA did relax some of the bans on tribal dances it did not relax the ban on Native American religions. This ban is still in effect today. The IRA also started the Indian Works Progress Administration or Indian WPA like to same program Roosevelt was using to put American back to work during the Great Depression. The Indian WPA was designed to help Indians start businesses and work in federally funded projects to upgrade the reservations and make them a better and more healthy place to live. Roosevelt looked the IRA over and wrote in the cover "Great Stuff" and then signed it into law on June 18, 1934.[15] A new beginning was coming now for many of the tribes in the United States.

Collier started right away with his Indian New Deal. The first order of business was to stop, and eventually Congress approved the repeal of, the Dawes Allotment Act of 1887; now, Indians could hold on to what little land they still had. Second, the government-run boarding school was to begin to be phased out and was by 1940, except for three schools that remain today, but as institutions for Indians as higher education schools. The Santa Fe Indian Industrial School in Santa Fe, New Mexico, is now the Institute of American Indian Art or IAIA, a fine arts college, the Haskell Indian School in Lawrence, Kansas, is now the First Nations Indian College, and the Riverside Indian School in Riverside, California, is now the Sherman Institute. But it was not until 1998 that all Catholic-affiliated Indian Schools were closed, and St. Catherine's Indian School in Santa Fe, New Mexico, was the last to close. Next, Collier started to work with the tribes to created new tribal governments that would give tribes their sovereignty back. There was only one catch to this part of the IRA and that was each tribal constitution had to be modeled after the U.S. Constitution. Controversy set in over this point in the IRA, and several tribes refused to take part in the IRA and the Indian WPA.[16]

One tribe that rejected the IRA was the Navajo. The tribal chairman at that time did not want the government-run boarding school system to stop and he did not want a tribal government modeled after the U.S. government. When the Navajo voted on the IRA, it was rejected, which came as a blow to Collier, since he had lived with the Pueblo and had worked many years with the Navajo as well.[17]

But there was another catch in the IRA and that was if the Commissioner of Indian Affairs desired, he could write the new Constitution for the tribe in question and force them to use that new Constitution. That is exactly what Collier did to the Navajo. Along with some other federal policies such as the sheep reduction program during the Dust Bowel years, Collier ordered the Navajo to reduce their sheep herds by one half to make sure there was enough grass to hold the top soil and keep it from blowing away. That policy created bitterness toward the memory of Collier and the federal government that still exists today. One thing to remember is that sheep become a part of the family as pets in Navajo culture, and killing the sheep was like killing a family member. Even though the IRA did give some ability to self-govern, only 173 tribes chose to participate, and seventy-three chose not to be included in the IRA. Even within the tribes that did accept the IRA, many votes were very close, most of the time 51 percent in favor to 49 percent opposed. Many tribal leaders said "We are given the ability to some self-government but why do we have to what Collier tells us to do."[18]

---

[14]Ronald Takaki, *A Different Mirror,* (New York: Little, Brown, and Company, 2008), 225.
[15]*Ibid.*
[16]*Ibid.*, 225–229.
[17]*Ibid.*
[18]*Ibid.*, 229.

The Indian WPA brought to the reservations something that was never present before: money and jobs. Many Indians have said "the Great Depression was the best time on the reservation."[19] From 1934 to 1938, many Indians on reservations were employed and had a lot of money to work with—something many of them had never had before. In the southwest in particular, the government helped many in the Pueblo, Navajo, and Hopi tribes to create craft-type businesses to market their art and jewelry making. But by 1936, the federal government had to enact the 1936 Arts and Crafts Act to protect Indians from these tribes from non-Indians making items and trying to market them as authentic Indian made. Many Americans were buying authentic Indian art and jewelry, and this venture was a way the U.S. government was hoping was a way for the tribes in the southwest to become more self-sustaining and eventually stop being dependent on the federal government. By 1940 though, it became evident that this program was not working. A major complaint from the Navajo Nation stated that 40 percent of the jobs on the Navajo Reservation were a government job of some sort. So the Navajo and other tribes were still dependent on the U.S. government for employment. Even though the tribes were able to exercise their tribal sovereignty, they were still wards of the government, still dependent on the government for money and jobs.[20]

© Reid Dalland/Shutterstock, Inc.

By 1938, the IRA and Indian WPA were defunded and disbanded. America was beginning to gear up to enter WWII but first had to help Great Britain through the Lend-Lease Act of 1938 to try to stop Hitler's march in Europe. Some Indians were able to find some employment off the reservations in the period 1938 to 1941 when the United States officially entered WWII, but most were still on the reservation. Even though Collier's ideas and changes were not perfect and exactly what many tribes wanted to see happen, it was a start. Tribes now had more control over their children's education, it was easier to market tribal art and jewelry, and the tribes had more ability to self-govern themselves and exhort tribal sovereignty, something that really never had been given to the Indians until now in the 1930s. But America's entry into the Second World War would bring even more changes to Indians in the United States.

World War Two

December 7, 1941, was a day of infamy according to Franklin D. Roosevelt. All Americans were caught off guard when the Japanese attacked Pearl Harbor on December 7, 1941. The Indians were a little upset with the attack as well, because they viewed that what little land they still had could be lost if the Japanese invaded the mainland United States. Many Indians volunteered to join the U.S. military and were accepted in. Things were

---

[19]*Ibid.*
[20]*Ibid.*, 225–229.

very different now, and many Indians were welcomed and many times fought in segregated units of Indians only with a white commander. Many Indian units fought in both Europe and in the Pacific.[21]

Most Indians now found less discrimination while serving in the military for the United States. It was the same way at home and on the reservations, now Indian women were taking on new roles in the absence of the men, and many Indian women found work in defense plants. For many Indians, this was the first time they were ever off the reservations and were discovering a new world away from the reservation. For many, they were making more money than they ever had in their lives and found new freedoms.[22]

Another group of Indians became very important to the war effort in the Pacific for the United States. They were known as the Navajo Code Talkers, and 400 Navajo young men volunteered to use their ancient language to help the United States. Just after the Pearl Harbor attack, the United States began its war effort against Japan. The first battles went very badly because the Japanese were able to break every code the U.S. was using in battle and the troops were being massacred.[23]

© Sue Stokes/Shutterstock, Inc.

Finally, the Marine Corps decided to go to the Navajo tribe and ask for volunteers to use the ancient Navajo language that the tribe used in battle. 400 Navajo volunteered to fight for the United States in 1942. The U.S. was in a desperate position in trying to fight the Japanese. It is an irony in history that the U.S. was asking for fluent speakers of the Navajo language, one of all of the tribal languages the U.S. was trying to obliterate starting in 1879 with Captain Henry Pratt until 1934 when the boarding school system was begun to be phased out. The 400 Navajo were very successful in the effort and helped win the war by 1945.[24]

After the war, many Indians did not return to the reservations and went on to other occupations in mainstream America. For women, it was different as with all women in the United States they had to give up the newfound independence they had tasted during the war while the men were gone to war. The Second World War brought about more change for Indians, both good and bad.[25]

The Disastrous Policy of Termination 1950 to 1952

By 1950, the U.S. government was looking at ways to get out of the Indian business. The government began to look at tribes very closely to see if there was a way each tribe had something they could call their own. Government officials wanted to know if a tribe could produce a product and become self-sustaining. With this, the tribes would have the ability to take care of themselves, without U.S. government assistance in the form of mainly commodities and certain government payments. As the government concluded its inquiry, it was determined that 109 Indian tribes had the ability to become self-sustaining.[26]

---

[21] *Ibid.*, 367–371.
[22] *Ibid.*, 367–371.
[23] *Ibid.*
[24] *Ibid.*
[25] *Ibid.*, 367–371.
[26] Anton Treuer. *Everything You Wanted to Know About Indians But Were Afraid to Ask* (St. Paul: Borealis Books, 2012), 99–106.

In Wisconsin, it was determined that the Menominee tribe had a solid lumbering business and they had over $7,000,000 dollars in a bank account. So in mid-1950, the Menominee were informed by the U.S. government that they would be terminated by mid-1952, thus giving the Menominee two years to prepare for the move to terminate their status as a recognized tribe by the United States.[27]

What is the Policy of Termination anyway? This is a policy the U.S. government came up which means that certain tribes were financially stable and had many of the tribal members working and were well off as well. All of this means that the United States was going to sever the tribal status of the Menominee tribe and 108 other tribes nationwide, making all tribal members just regular citizens of the United States that the United States now had no finical responsibility to. To protect their land, the Menominee petitioned the State of Wisconsin for their reservation, which was going to disappear in 1952, to become the 72nd county of Wisconsin. In early 1952, the Wisconsin State Legislature passed a bill and the Governor of Wisconsin signed it into law, making the Menominee tribe's reservation the 72nd county in Wisconsin: called Menominee County.[28]

On the surface, this move by the United Sates looks like a very good move as a way to get out of the Indian business. The Menominee had a thriving sustainable lumbering industry and had money in the bank. But two year after the Policy of Termination took effect in 1952, by 1954, Menominee County was now the poorest county in Wisconsin and the tribe had to sell some of its tribal land in order to pay some outstanding property taxes owed to Wisconsin.[29]

One item the federal government overlooked was that all citizens of the tribe became subject to state laws and several taxes that the Menominee were not previously subject to. Another fact that the U.S. government overlooked was that although the Menominee had built a highly successful lumber business in the previous 200 years, the biggest customer was U.S. government with their contracts, which now the Menominee had to compete for and bid against other lumber companies.[30]

© symbiot/Shutterstock, Inc.

The situation for the Menominee did not get any better as time went on. By the mid-1960s, the tribe was not only the poorest county in Wisconsin, they were fairly close to being the poorest tribe in the United States. By 1970, the unthinkable happened, the Menominee lost the hospital they had in Keshena, leaving them with no affordable health care and soon rioting and protests started. A Menominee woman named Ada Deer took

---

[27]Patty Loew. *Indian Nations of Wisconsin: Histories of Endurance and Renewal,* (Madison: Wisconsin Historical Press, 2013), 30–37.
[28]Treuer, 99–106 and Loew 30–37.
[29]Loew, 30–37.
[30]*Ibid.*

the initiative to try to get the Policy of Termination reversed. She worked in Washington, D.C., and eventually was appointed to President Richard Nixon's cabinet. There she worked hard to get the disastrous Termination policy reversed. Finally in 1972, Nixon reviewed everything that had occurred to the Menominee since the Termination policy had taken effect in 1952 and determined that the policy had forever hurt and set back the Menominee tribe. As it turned out, it was cheaper to allow the Menominee tribe to keep their tribal status and receive the government commodities and payments. It was costing the federal government more in welfare payments to individual Menominee tribal members than to keep them as a recognized tribe and to pay what the U.S. government owed the tribe from previous agreements.[31]

In 1972, Nixon reinstated the Menominee tribe's status as a federally recognized tribe. But it has been a very long road to recovery. The tribe became so poor it still took 40+ years to recover, and still today have not fully regained their prominence and wealth they possessed before 1952. By 1956, the U.S. government came up with another idea and program for Indians to become more self-sustaining: The Urban Relocation Act of 1956.[32]

Urban Relocation and Coming Together Resist

1956 brought a new program to try to get Indians off the reservations and into mainstream American life. The Urban Relocation Act of 1956 offered any Indian living on the reservation a one-way bus ticket to an urban center, like Minneapolis, Los Angles, New York City, and Cleveland. What the program offered was after arriving in the urban area the government would have a place for them to live and thirty days of job training. After the training period, the people that were relocated would be able to find a job and become self-sustaining, getting them off the government tribal payment welfare rolls.[33]

© happycreator/Shutterstock, Inc.

The Urban Relocation Program had many good intentions but was not the program that was promised. Many Indians went to the urban areas expecting to become self-sustaining. But when they arrived, what they found was either no housing as promised or being put up in a low-budget hotel in the middle of a ghetto in a large city. Often times, there was no job training or a job waiting to be filled. The Indian people that participated in the Relocation Program found themselves competing with other minorities, African Americans,

[31]*Ibid.*, 30–37.
[32]*Ibid.*
[33]*Ibid.*, 97–98.

Hispanics, and low-income whites for jobs. By 1958, about half of the participants went back to the reservations, because they believed they were worse off in the inner city than back on the reservation.[34]

For the Indians that stayed in the inner cities, something else began to happen that was an unintended outcome that the U.S. government did not expect to happen. The program had brought together many Indians from many different tribes. They all one thing on common from their boarding school days, and that was that the all spoke English. As the Indians from different tribes walked around in the inner cities, they all recognized each other and eventually began to communicate about problems they were encountering and how to deal with such problems. Relocation was a failure for the U.S. government, but was a success for the Indians that stayed in the inner city and did not return to the reservations.[35]

The Indians that stayed now began to from pressure groups and help groups to deal with everyday problems they encountered. These Indians bean to make their demands heard at the local government level, and they started movements to regain everything Indians had lost over the previous 500 years. The most radical group that was formed was the American Indian Movement (AIM) in Minneapolis, Minnesota.[36]

AIM started as the Red Patrol, a group that would walk to streets of Minneapolis to protect Indians from police harassment and other attacks by other people on young Indians and tribal Elders that were living in Minneapolis in 1968. Even though for the most part the Relocation Program was a failure for the U.S. government, the program was an avenue for Indians to finally bring to the forefront, to the U.S. people and the world, their problems and mistreatment.[37]

Alcatraz 1969 to 1971 and Wounded Knee 1973

The first attempt to occupy Alcatraz Island in San Francisco Bay was in 1964. A small band of Indians from the San Francisco area went out to the island and set up camp. Their demands were simple, they wanted an Indian Education Center, a Tribal College, and a museum to tell the truth of how contact with Europeans and Americans had forever changed the lives of the Indians. The siege lasted three days, and at that point the Indians occupying Alcatraz left peacefully as nobody noticed they were out on the island.[38]

© Sawasdee Snap/Shutterstock, Inc.

---

[34]*Ibid.*
[35]*Ibid.*, 109–110.
[36]*Ibid.*
[37]*Ibid.*
[38]*Ibid.*

Alcatraz is an interesting place as most Americans know it from the days it was a maximum security prison, from the 1930s to 1960 when it was closed. It was built to house the gangsters that were common during the 1930s crime spree. Originally, Alcatraz was a home to some California Indians. When the band of Indians took over Alcatraz in 1964, they were also reclaiming some lost land.[39]

In 1969, amid the social restlessness in the United States, a group of Indian students from both the University of California Berkeley and San Francisco State University, decided to take and occupy Alcatraz Island and make it into an Indian museum, Tribal College, and Indian Cultural and Educational Center. Soon, The American Indian Movement also joined the siege, but AIM had many contacts to media outlets and the Indians were on the evening news nearly every night. As the siege wore on, the federal government cut the media access, the water supply, and the electricity. Soon, the united front collapsed and infighting broke out among different Indian groups. By 1971, the united front was splintering. As conditions became worse, with no water and lack of food, the siege was quickly coming to an end. What brought the siege to an end was when Richard Oaks's, a founder and leader of AIM, daughter fell mysteriously down a stairway and died. Oaks left the next day and the siege ended by the end of the week.[40]

AIM was involved in several other acts of resistance and violence over the years. In 1972, the high point was the occupation and trashing of the Bureau of Indian Affairs Office Building in Washington, D.C., during the summer. At this point in the history of AIM, the Federal Justice Department viewed AIM to be just as dangerous as the Black Panthers. AIM was in Washington to protest and bring attention to all of the broken treaties between the Indian Tribes and the United States. They had arranged with the Department of the Interior to have camping space on the Washington Mall that is between the Washington Monument and the Capital Building. Upon arriving, the Indians were told no arrangements were made for them and asked to leave. The Indians became very angry and decided to take over the BIA building instead to make their point. What happened after the takeover, trashing the building and with many important documents dealing with treaties and other information dealing with the relationships between the federal government, caused the image of AIM to tarnish a great deal. Again, fracturing among groups within AIM caused the takeover to fall apart and after seven days the AIM left Washington. It would be only eight short months later that AIM would again be on the center stage again, only this time the entire world would be watching and AIM and Indian people everywhere in the United States would finally after 500 years get to explain their plight and the entire world would now see how the American Indian was really being treated.[41]

© sevenMaps7/Shutterstock, Inc.

[39]*Ibid.*
[40]*Ibid.*
[41]*Ibid.*

In late January and early February 1973, the Oglala Sioux on the Pine Ridge Reservation were trying to oust Dick Wilson, a corrupt tribal leader that was favoring the more assimilated Indians living on the reservation than the more traditional Lakota living on the reservation. The Lakota had held a referendum election to try to vote out Wilson, but to no avail. Wilson won by bribing and intimidating several tribal members who owed him favors to vote for him. Oglala now was asking the Bureau of Indian Affairs and the Department of the Interior for an investigation on corruption on their reservation. The agencies refused to do so, and the Oglala were left no other option but to ask AIM for help.[42]

AIM arrived on the night of February 22, 1973. They took over the trade post on the Pine Ridge Reservation and the church. At first, the news reported that AIM had taken hostages but that turned out to be false. AIM had and used all of their media outlets, and the Indians holding the town were on the news every night both in the United States and around the world.[43]

Many things happened at Wounded Knee. Indians were able to state their gripes and problems with the United States on a daily basis. The siege posed several problems for the United States. Wounded Knee was the last place of armed resistance and had ended in a massacre of 300 Lakota men, women, and children in December 1890 at the hands of the U.S. Army. The U.S. could ill afford another massacre at the same place just eighty-three years later. The United States went on full alert right after the siege began. They mobilized the U.S. Marshalls, the South Dakota State Police, the National Guard, and the U.S. Army and Air Force. The Air Force was routinely running low-level strafing moves, but not shooting daily. The Indians holding Wounded Knee figured that the Air Force would sooner or later drop napalm on them and kill all of them.[44]

Weaponry the Indians possessed were only hunting rifles and shotguns, contrary to what the United States said they had. They only had one AK-47 that had no ammunition, and so was never used. On the other hand, the U.S. forces had high powered military weapons and shot over 500,000 rounds of ammunition at Wounded Knee. It is surprising that only two Indians were killed, but several were wounded. AIM and the other Indians from all over the United States were willing to die and expected the United States to kill all of them because this is what had happened in the past. The U.S. could not afford to allow this to happen because the entire world was watching.[45]

Something else that was very special happened at Wounded Knee. Of the protesters and other Indians that came to Wounded Knee, at its peak there were 2,000 Indians holding up in Wounded Knee. Over half of the Indians were Urban Indians, a product of the Urban Relocation Act of 1956. These Indians were either relocated Indians or the children of relocated Indians and had lost all contact with their tribal heritage. When these Urban Indians arrived at Wounded Knee, there were many traditional Indians living on Pine Ridge Reservation, and the traditional Indians and Elders at Pine Ridge Reservation erected Sweat Lodges to purify and welcome back the Urban Indians that had lost their way.[46]

The Sweat Lodge is a central part of both Lakota and Ojibwe religions. It is designed to purify a person's body and used to commemorate a special event. Sweats are used to commemorate a young man's successful vision quest or to find your purpose in life. A sweat is used when a young woman comes of age to celebrate that she is now a giver of life. Sweats are not done with men and women together. A Medicine Man conducts the all-male sweat and a Medicine Woman conducts the all-female sweat. Men and Women do not sweat together. The Sweat Lodge ceremony is an important part of all Indian cultures and societies, and is a way they come closer to the Creator and keep themselves pure.[47]

---

[42]*Ibid.*
[43]*Ibid.*
[44]*Ibid.*
[45]*Ibid.*
[46]*Ibid.*
[47]*Ibid.*

The returning Urban Indians also were learning other aspects of their culture they had lost, things like the use of tobacco and how to use the pipe and how to conduct the Pipe Ceremony. Here was probably was the most important item that came out of Wounded Knee, the cultural revitalization of American Indian culture. All of the lost souls were now coming home and needed to be taught about and reclaim their cultural heritage. The returning Indians learned about tobacco ties and their use. A tobacco tie is a 2 inch square piece of red cloth that has a small amount of tobacco placed in the center. Then the opposite corners are taken and brought to the top in the center and all four corners are tied together with a white ribbon. A tobacco tie is placed at sacred sites of the Indians and also is given to an Elder if you are asking for his wisdom on an issue or problem in life. Tobacco is a sacred item in Indian culture, and tobacco ties and the pipe are gifts given from the Creator and have to be held in the highest esteem.[48]

Something else dramatic happened at Wounded Knee as well. Halfway through the siege, the Oglala declared themselves an independent nation separate from the United States. They called their state the Independent Oglala Lakota Nation, and directly went to the United Nations in New York to present their case of human rights violations committed by the United States against the Lakota and all Indian people. The Lakota were not allowed a chance to speak in front of the General Assembly of the U.N., but the international press coverage was enough to give their cause creditability.[49]

[48]*Ibid.*
[49]*Ibid.*

Finally in May of 1973, the second Indian fatality of the siege happened. Many of the Indians called the death cold-blooded murder by the federal troops that surrounded Wounded Knee, because the man had his back to the man that shot him and killed him. After his funeral, the Lakota Traditional leaders said enough is enough and called for the end of the siege. The siege ended, but Dick Wilson was still in power. Over the next several years, Wilson killed all of his opposition on the Pine Ridge Reservation and life went back to the way it was before the seventy-one-day siege.[50]

After Wounded Knee 1973

Wounded Knee 1973 can be looked at as a successful failure. First, the siege was a failure in that Dick Wilson retained power and killed all of his opposition without any prosecution. He was never charged with anything. There was no immediate change in federal Indian policy either as was hoped as the world discovered what was happening to American Indians. But what was not expected was that as the American public was following the siege on television, 71 percent sided with the Indians after they understood the issues that had plagued them for the last 200+ years. Americans had discovered that Indians really did still exist as almost all Americans had believed that Indians had disappeared sometime before 1900. It was a real awakening for the American public. A new public outcry began to help Indians in one way or another. One of the demands of the Indians holding Wounded Knee was again to gain more control of the education of their children. Eventually this would happen, but it was a few years in the future. The Indians holding got help from another unexpected place, and that was Hollywood. Marlin Brando refused his Academy Award for best actor for his role in the *Godfather*. He was not present but sent a young Apache woman named Silverfeather to refuse the award and express his displeasure of how Indians were depicted in Hollywood movies. He also said he would go to Wounded Knee, but never made it there.[51]

AIM had several problems after the siege at Wounded Knee. Congressional hearings and several court appearances eventually broke AIM, and it was never as radical a group again. But AIM still exists. They are located in Minneapolis, Minnesota, and help Indians living in the urban setting find legal help, housing, and education, and help solve many other problems Indians face today.[52]

The successes that came out of Wounded Knee 1973 were many, and they came at a reasonable pace during the 1970s and 1980s. Another demand AIM wanted was more control over the education of Indian children and cultural education. In the mid-1970s, AIM pioneered the first Indian school devoted to cultural education. The school, *Heart of the Earth Survival School*, in Minneapolis, was the first K-12 Tribal Cultural School in the United States. Many more have followed since this school opened.[53]

Other revitalization programs include language preservation. The Ojibwe and Navajo tribes are the leaders in this area. They do this through immersion schools. The Indian children all speak English, so at the immersion they are immersed in their native language. Language preservation is of high importance to Native Americans because when Columbus came to the Americans over 500 Native American languages existed, but today there are only 180 left, and over half of them are at risk of disappearing.[54] It is very important to Indian tribes because according to archeologists and anthropologists when a language dies the culture dies as well. No tribe wants that to happen to them, and that is why they are seeking out as many as they can first speakers. The Ojibwe at Red Lake Reservation in Minnesota have the most

---

[50]*Ibid.*

[51]*Ibid.*

[52]*Ibid.*

[53]Treuer, 110.

[54]*Ibid.*, 79–85.

speakers and they work with the young children to learn the language.[55] The Ojibwe language is difficult to learn and is very expressive of Ojibwe culture. The language gives the worldview of the tribe and distinguishes between what is alive and what is not alive. It is a very complex language, but progress is being made, as is with all language preservation efforts. It is hoped that some languages have not passed the point of no return.[56]

One other cultural revitalization effort is the return to the Native American traditional diet. The issue is relative new. Because many Native people were forced to change their diet, many became sick with Type II Diabetes. The problem occurred because Native Americans did not grow or eat wheat, they ate corn, beans, and squash, or the "Three Sisters." When Native people return to the traditional diet, they had a miraculous turnaround in health. Seventy percent had their medications reduced, and half of that 70 percent went off their medications in six months. The issue is a new one Native Communities are facing today, and more research is coming in on this issue. It is amazing what happens when Indians go back to their indigenous knowledge. They know how to survive and how to live healthy.[57]

Over the last 500+ years, Native Americans have changed and altered their lifestyles for both Europeans and Americans. They lost nearly all of their land, culture, and language. They survived the American Policy of Extermination of the late nineteenth century. They survived the "Save the Indian" campaign of the Progressive Era. They and their languages survived the boarding school system the United States put in place to try to kill Native culture and language and make young children forget their tribe, parents, customs, and culture. It did not work; the Indians are still here and revitalizing their culture and language. The Indians were able to come back, and are coming back. There are still issues, like the Black Hills and the Lakota, and regaining sacred sites that were lost over the years while the Indians were confined to the reservations. The story of the Native Americans is one of the greatest comeback stories of all time. To have numbers in the tens of millions before Columbus arrived, to a low of 237,196 by 1900, and then to come back and reclaim their culture and begin to educate their children through culture education: The story of the American Indian is by far the greatest comeback story of all time.

© Eric Kukulowicz/Shutterstock, Inc.

Works Cited

LaDuke, Winona. *Recovering the Sacred The Power of Naming and Claiming*, Cambridge: South End Press, 2005.

Larner, John W. Jr., ed. *The Papers of the Society of American Indians* parts 1 and 2. Wilmington DE: Scholarly Resources, 1987. Microfilm.

Loew, Patty. *Indian Nations of Wisconsin: Histories of Endurance and Renewal*, Madison: Wisconsin Historical Press, 2013.

McGerr, Michael. *A Fierce Discontent: The Rise and Fall or the Progressive Movement In America*, New York: Oxford University Press, 2003.

The Meriam Report: The Problem of Indian Administration, National Indian Law Library. https://narf.org/nill/resources/meriam.html (accessed: October 10, 2014).

---

[55]*Ibid.*, 79–85.

[56]*Ibid.*

[57]Winona LaDuke, *Recovering the Sacred The Power of Naming and Claiming* (Cambridge: South End Press, 2005), 153–210.

Montezuma, Carlos. Gale Encyclopedia of Biography, Answers.com. http://answers.com/topic/montezuma-carlos (accessed January 15, 2014).

Stout, Mary A. *Native American Boarding Schools,* Santa Barbara: Greenwood, 2012.

Takaki, Ronald. *A Different Mirror,* New York: Little, Brown, and Company, 2008.

Treuer, Anton. *Everything You Wanted to Know About Indians But Were Afraid to Ask.* St. Paul: Borealis Books, 2012.

PBS, "The American Experience: We Shall Remain: Wound Knee," 2009, Films on Demand McIntyre Library University of Wisconsin-Eau Claire (accessed March 30, 2015).